THE BLESSING

New and Selected Poems

RICHARD JONES

The Blessing

New and Selected Poems

COPPER CANYON PRESS

Copper Canyon Press is in residence under the auspices of the Centrum
Foundation at Fort Worden State Park in Port Townsend, Washington.
Centrum sponsors artist residences, education workshops for Washington
State students and teachers, blues, jazz, and fiddle tunes festivals, classical
music performances, and The Port Townsend Writers' Conference.

LIBRARY OF CONGRESS CATALOGING-IN-PUBLICATION DATA
Jones, Richard, 1953–
The blessing: new and selected poems / by Richard Jones.
p.   cm.
ISBN 1-55659-142-X (alk. paper)
ISBN 1-55659-143-8 (pbk.: alk. paper)
1. Title. PS3560.O52475 B58 2000
811'.54—DC21
CIP

COPPER CANYON PRESS
Post Office Box 271
Port Townsend, Washington 98368
www.coppercanyonpress.org

for all of us

ACKNOWLEDGMENTS

AGNI, All Things Considered (National Public Radio), *American Poetry
Review, Another Chicago Magazine, The Arts Journal, BBC Radio*
(The British Broadcasting Company, London), *Bluff City, Chariton Review,
Cimarron Review, Conduit, Columbia Poetry Review, Crazyhorse,
Cream City Review, Crosscurrents, Dial-a-Poem Chicago!, Empty Shelves,
Graham House Review, Green Mountains Review, Hubbub, Iris,
Kansas Quarterly, Luna, Manhattan Poetry Review, Mānoa,
New American Poets of the 90s* (Godine), *New Letters, Northern Lights,
ONTHEBUS, Osiris, Pembroke Magazine, Pequod, Poet Lore, Poetry,
Poetry Chronicle* (India), *Poetry-in-Motion, Poetry Now, Power Lines*
(Tia Chucha Press), *Quarry West, The Quarterly, Rhino, The Seattle Review,
Second Street Anthology, Silverfish Review, smartish pace, Spillway,
Third Coast, TriQuarterly, Virginia Quarterly Review,
Willow Springs, Zone 3*

Some of the poems in this volume were originally published in *Country of Air*
(1986), *At Last We Enter Paradise* (1991), *A Perfect Time* (1994), and
48 Questions (1998). Other poems in this collection were published in the
following limited editions:

Windows and Walls (Adastra Press, 1982)

Innocent Things (Adastra Press, 1985)

Walk On (Alderman Press, 1986)

Sonnets (Adastra Press, 1991)

The Abandoned Garden (The Nomadic Press, 1997)

48 Questions (A Tebot Bach Book, 1998)

The Stone It Lives On (Adastra Press, 2000)

Contents

Country of Air (1986)

At Last We Enter Paradise (1991)

PART TWO

A Perfect Time (1994)

48 Questions (1998)

Paintings (2000)

The Blessing (2000)

THE BLESSING

New and Selected Poems

Country of Air

The Bell

In the tower the bell
is alone, like a man
in his room,
thinking and thinking.

The bell is made of iron.
It takes the weight
of a man
to make the bell move.

Far below, the bell feels
hands on a rope.
It considers this.
It turns its head.

Miles away,
a man in his room
hears the clear sound,
and lifts his head to listen.

PART ONE

Times Like This

Child in Woods

From inside my house I hear,
across the pasture, beyond the lake,
a boy hidden in pine woods
screaming, "goddamn, goddamn."
It's my neighbor's boy,
an angel-faced kid of eight,
yelling at the world.

I know those woods well.
Sunlight pours down through the branches
stained yellow and green and warm as love.
In those woods, a man
can walk out of the shadow of his life
and stand in shafts of sunlight,
the body numinous.

But the child is screaming.
What does he care that the day is perfect?
He's falling in a frenzy to the forest floor,
rolling around on soft pine needles,
pretending, screaming, killing some animal
only he can see.

I listen to the boy for a long time.
And though I know he'll soon rise up,
exhausted, his demons departed,
though I know he'll return home,
pine dust in his hair,
to the ones who worship him,

who make their home a temple
for the living paradise which is childhood,
though I know he is just a boy,
I can't help but hear

the man in the child's voice,
the man who invites his troubles,
his screaming like a prayer,
an invocation, calling the pain
which will come, and by which
his life will be defined.

The Wounded One

Geese crossing the cornfields,
gunshots coming from the woods,
the sky changing from blue to red
as the sun goes down. Geese cry out
and keep flying. I see them running
from gunfire, jostling one another,
sticking together, bound to one another
by fear and love and history. One bird
drops out of the V, calling out, like the others,
who turn as one for a moment, then rise again
to cross the ridge, leaving the wounded one behind.
She drops, flies low, struggling past my garden,
where I stand watching as she flies to the lake.
I hear her falling into the water,
hear men and dogs in the woods,
birds calling to one another beyond the ridge.
I cross the field to the lake,
following the cries of the bird,
and find her in the shallows of the marsh grass,
head held high, water stained red, her body
pushing itself around in circles.
I wade into the water, cold water, and hear
my breath coming faster. She hears it
and tries to lift up onto the opposite shore.
I'm coming to save her, or to bury her.
But she is alive,
and terrified.
She retreats into the woods,

farther and farther away.
She is determined to live,
to see this life through, until it's finished.

The Birds

When I try to say something about the birds
living around my house, or about the jay
tearing the cold insides from a mouse
I killed and tossed in the yard,
I find myself writing instead
about Anne, the secretary I knew
in New York. She was afraid of people.
Even when the phone rang,
she'd sometimes start crying
and lock herself in the ladies' room.

I bet Anne could write a poem about the birds
for me. She'd know what to say
about the cream-colored bird I saw yesterday,
the way it made me think not about birds,
how they starve in winter,
but about the life of the soul.

I'd like to know what happened to crazy Anne.
The last time I saw her was in Times Square, after work.
Snow was falling and for once she wasn't crying.
She said, "My best friend's been murdered."
She was staring at neon reflecting
on the wet pavement, the snow
falling as in a dream, repeating
the dead girl's name over and over,
the same as hers,
Anne, Anne....

The Mechanic

It's dark in the garage. The mechanic
goes down into the concrete grave
with his trouble light, while the day
rushes past outside on the highway.

Standing in the pit beneath an old engine,
he works patiently, with a kind of gentleness.
Looking up, he could be in a field at night
staring into the sky for answers.

In the afternoon, when the owners come back
for their cars, he stands around with the other men,
drinking beer, pushing one another around, cursing.
He works the kinks out of his neck, squints into the sun.

The Letter

The clerk in the post office stops
one minute, lays down
a handful of letters on the table
before the wall of wooden letter slots.

He removes his glasses and wipes them
with a handkerchief pulled from his pocket.
When he breathes on the glass,
he can see the fingerprint of the world.

As he cleans his glasses he thinks
of his son, of the boy's last letter,
the casual way he wrote, "Tomorrow
I'm going back to the front."

Today the country is at peace.
The clerk resumes his work.
He reads each envelope, the names
of strangers, and each minute

his grief begins again,
holding letters in his hand,
feeling them moving through the world,
breathless and white.

Mrs. Green

I opened and let her in —
Mrs. Green, our elderly neighbor,
drunk again and knocking on the door.
She wanted to nap on our sofa.
Her dressing gown open, I saw
how mournfully her empty breasts hung down.
Taking my arm to steady herself,
she called me by her husband's name.
He loved her, but didn't let her drink.
He hid the keys to her car.
Some nights I heard them arguing.
Often she went to the hospital.
The doctors put her back together
whenever she broke herself.

It's funny. Mr. Green
died years before she did.
She kept going.
She sleeps in my memory on our sofa.
And still inside her is the deep
fear and knowledge
that another night is coming,
the cold and the shaking.
Some nights I looked down
from my window, saw her
crawling around in the dark,
digging in our backyard for bottles she hid.
Looking up at my face and howling,
it seemed to me, when she found nothing.

Bread Crumbs

They knock with their Bibles
on your grandmother's front door.
One man presses his fat red face
against the screen, yelling,

but he can't see you.
The two of you
are a secret behind the sofa.
It's a little game

your grandmother has taught you:
when a salesman comes
you play silence and hiding
and no money.

Your grandmother knows the virtue of patience.
The man on the porch will go away.
So you wait like a child waiting, head bowed,
for a prayer to end, when all you want

is to eat supper with her,
and, afterward, sweep the table clean
the way she showed you,
one hand brushing bread crumbs into the other—

both hands filled,
just enough in each fist to open
the door and face the hungry day.

The Spiders

It took my father and me years to learn
how to talk. Now we don't say anything.
We touch each other from a distance,
two men carrying a ladder
we set against his house.

Along the coast, people live
in houses built on stilts,
so when storms rage up the shore
the ocean passes safely underneath.

Spiders live there, too,
working their webs each day.
In one evening
they can cover the house
while he's inside, sleeping,
sprawled across the bed
as though he'd fallen there by accident
to finish the day.

When I visit my father,
we cover our faces with rags.
We mix poison.
I can't turn away,
holding the ladder so my father doesn't fall,
and, as he climbs away from me,
as I forgive us both,

I see that we have found
ourselves at last—
me on the earth, my father in the sky—
and I don't turn away from the spiders
or the poison blessing this house.

The Idle Fleet

James River, Virginia

The river below hard as steel,
a boy stands on the deck
of a mothballed battleship
and feels the wind in his hair.
He isn't thinking about history
and war. He doesn't care
that what saved us
has become old and useless,
each ship its own gray tombstone
anchored in the James.
It is enough for him
to be alive, to challenge
the other boys rowing out
to climb into the sky.
He knows it is better,
now, while he is alive,
not to think but to fling
himself into the air
and go flying,
become an angel,
let the simple air hold him
like the hand of God
until he falls,
with the others,
exploding into the water,
the dirty river accepting him
in its current, carrying him
into the future,
into his life as a man.

Riding the Train

Floating toward home, through the window
I see towns built around churches,
the dead a field of fenced-in names,
the blank stare of the stones;
and now, between church and cemetery,
the faces of children in a garden
who've stopped to watch the train pass through,
out into fields and open places.
There I see a pickup turn off the main road
and lose itself in a gold cloud.
At the end of the lane, a woman
lives alone in a farmhouse.
She feels the earth trembling, the train
going by like a moment of anger.
She leans toward the window to see,
one hand parting the curtain,
one hand gripping the wheel of her chair.

Times Like This

She closes the gate
of the public garden
behind her, an autumn garden,
walled-in, without flowers,
only bare fruit trees
and the intimation
of bad weather.
I'm by myself on the bench,
the leaves, like the children
we talked about having,
racing back and forth
in the windy sunshine
at my feet. It's a scene
we know by heart —
the careful voices,
the careful good-byes.
We've learned it is better
not to talk at times like this
but to leave quietly when
we must, the only sound
the click of a lock.
The afternoon caught
between apple trees
twisted in thought
and pomegranates blooming
along the north wall,
I see she's gone for good.
I count the minutes,
the bricks in the wall,

the money I'll need next week,
the children we won't have.
This small garden
is the perfect size
for my angry heart,
for all the dark words
that created this silence,
for the emptiness
which will survive
in the solitude of desire,
and for the rough grace
which illuminates the soul,
poised between love and nothing.

The Fire

While the man next door rests in bed,
it begins:
the moment in the wiring gnawed by a mouse.
Flame opens like a seed, so small
it's almost impossible to see
even in the dark, even if you
were standing in the room
listening for the spark.
But no matter how small, fire
loves wood. It fills the rooms
with smoke the sleepers inhale,
smoke taking them deeper.

Next door, the man turns in bed,
then sits up.
He goes to the window.
He goes outside. The neighbor's house
sings with fire, light
dances in his face. He can't believe
what he sees
although someday he'll understand
how often this happens,
the infinite number
of lives and deaths he's slept through.

PART TWO

Country of Air

A Suicide

A few minutes ago,
on the roof,
she believed she had become
light enough to go dancing
in the country of air.
She imagined a hand
reaching out to her.
It was, finally, all she wanted.

On the street, people
turn away from the body,
her back broken
across the top of the fence.
They see her
as a worn-out coat
left behind on the iron railing,
forgotten by some silly girl
gone dancing.
The way her legs dangle down
it is easy to imagine

she was dancing.
The peaceful look on her face
makes it possible to believe
she is exhausted,
and sleeping now,
were it not for the fact
her eyes are slightly open,
seeming to see us.

The Gift

I've given you nothing
today, or yesterday, so tonight
I go out to the graveyard
in the rain to pick

the spring's first wildflowers—
daffodils a century old
growing wild over the graves.
I bend down and think of you

alone in the bed
and confess what I love:
darkness and the desire
to lie down here forever.

What have I to give anyone?
Even these stupid flowers
seem like a dead man's fist,
holding on and never letting go.

The Solipsist's Self-Portraits

1. THE BED

Drunk under the blanket,
sheet pulled over my head —
the bed becomes my cloud,
floating high above you,
who are calling me back.
You say I am lost,
but I know where I am:
on a cloud so far away
no one can touch me,
no one can hurt me
because I'm not human:
I'm a deaf angel,
someone who will never hear you
or speak to you again.

2. PORTRAIT OF A MAN WALKING

Look how gracefully he moves,
strolling down the street
like a cloud, slipping
between people, past cars.
Even when faces rush forward
to greet him, he smiles,
and moves on, effortlessly,
like a ghost walking
through a wall, his life
falling away behind him,

a wake, a jetsam of facts
in an ocean of faces
he believes, he believes,
he's touched.

3. THE LIE

I am telling you a lie,
a great lie that goes on and on,
a lie as huge as a life,
a lie as strong as planks
lining the hull of a ship,
a lie as sharp as the ax
that cuts the ropes
tied to the dock,
a lie as tall and empty
as the black sails
carrying me out to sea.
The lie is the captain
standing on the deck,
I, his prisoner,
locked in the hold.
The bars on the porthole frame
people gathered on the shore.
They are so far away I know
I will never see them again.
If they could hear me
I swear I'd tell the truth
this time, truth blooming
like a white rose
so beautiful no one would believe it.

But everyone is growing smaller,
a little bouquet in the distance.
They can't hear me,
or my plea to be forgiven,
or the last thing I said:
Take me back.

Cloudburst

Black shadows descend
on the garden
of tulips and daffodils

and Mother runs down
the farmhouse steps,
her hand on her dress,

to save the white sheet
waving on the line.
It wants to blow away,

to fall into the dirt
where rain and earth
will wear it

to nothing,
a rag.
But Mother hugs

the bedclothes tight,
like a baby she carries
into the house.

From far away
she calls
my name.

I see her
brush the raindrops
from her thick black hair.

Looking at My Father

When I come down
after searching for him in the attic
among the uniforms and the flight gear
to find him digging in his garden,
I don't see a pilot, I see a farmer,
a solid man built for standing on the earth.

He spent a lifetime flying,
but never talks about it,
the way a man won't tell his wife
of the mistress he once loved,
the secret story of his life,
what came between them.

My father's eyes are a faint blue,
the color of sky fading into nothing.
I imagine him looking down at us
from his country of air.
We are so small
from that great distance.

Wings

I loved the wings
on his flight jackets—
silver wings
I'd hold in my hand,
a silver star
where the heart should have been.
As a child,
I used to climb trees
to find him.
Trees are what I imagined
wings felt like
waving all around me.
I'd reach the top
and wait all day
for one white line
written in the sky,
for distant silver wings
to echo the sun,
the silence so bright
it hurt to look.

The Danger of Escaping

Sometimes I go too high,
sometimes I float out
beyond the white rope
that my body,
far below on the earth,
is patiently holding.
I barely can see
myself down there,
the husk of my flesh,
the heavy damp feel
of my skin, the way
I lie on my back
like a dead man
saying my name.
This is when I know
it is useless: I've gone
so high and so far
I'm afraid
I'll never come back.

Waiting

I've been waiting here so long
I've forgotten what it is I'm waiting for.
I've forgotten why I wait by the window
watching the road and listening.

Maybe someone's come already?
Maybe I hid in my room
when I heard the footsteps?
Maybe I'm not waiting, but hiding?

Or maybe it's impossible to hide
and someone is here with me now.
Maybe I'm already holding everyone in my arms
I'll ever love, or know, or be.

The Insects

When I write
the insects come
to bother me.
They dance in the light.
They make love,
their little wings
singing to one another.
But I have work to do.
I brush them away.
I don't mean to kill anyone,
but sometimes their bodies
leave brown smudges
on the paper under my hands.
You can't see this,
reading what I've written,
now, in this book.

For My Friends

Days are spent in the meadow brooding
over lives that go on without me

in the city. Friends meet
after work in bars and talk
about music and Marx and what is wrong
with American men. It is still light
when they go out among the crowds
on Columbus Avenue, walking uptown
to the Mexican restaurant, where the service is slow,
and you can sit all night in the courtyard
while empty plates pile up around you,
and night covers the square of sky
above you, and lights come on
everywhere, and the city is

alive, like this meadow in summer —
a million small things buzzing with life —
as I make my way back to the farmhouse in the dark.

Life after Death

What I envy in the open eyes
of the dead deer hanging down
from the rafters, its eyes
still wet and glassy, but locked now
into a vision of another life,
is the way it seems to be
staring at the moment when
it died. The blue light
falling through the window
into this smoke-filled room
is the same color as the mist
coming down off the mountain
that morning: the deer sees
men with guns,
but also sees, beyond them,
the endless mountains.

PART THREE

Paradise on Fire

A Boy's Body

He has a perfect body, this boy
in a checkered bathing suit
walking away from me
toward the lake,
his waist hard and slim as a girl's,
the muscular back and broad shoulders
already strong enough to bear sorrow and grief.
God knows what he's thinking about
as he strolls toward the water.
He sees, across the pasture,
two horses coming toward him.
His small heart—
people pound on the walls
to get in, to get out.
It makes him walk
a little awkwardly.
Like Michelangelo's *David*,
he has big feet
and large delicate hands.
When the hill slopes down
he picks up speed, begins to run,
his body gaining power,
almost beyond his control,
enough to kill,
or touch us with his love.

The Horses

The rain has come
and I cannot see the three horses
wandering in the pasture.
It's logical
to say they are still there,
huddled under the trees,
the rain turning to mist
as it falls through the branches.
I know nothing about horses
except that they will come back,
waiting for me by the fence,
bowing their sad and beautiful faces,
wanting to kiss my hand.
They stand all winter in silence.
It's like a dream I don't understand.
I walk outside and see,
as the rain turns to snow,
these slow, lumbering horses
moving toward me,
the heavy walk
toward apples and sugar,
their heads hung low
with that miserable look
I somehow love
but have never loved enough.

The Miscarriage

The day we lost the baby
and I came home
to find you
drugged, in pain,
the white nightgown
delicately shrouding your body,
I sat in the chair
at the foot of the iron bed
and listened to you cry.
I did not say much
except that it would be all right,
then cradled my arms carefully around you.
What did I know?
As I held you,
I felt I had been caught.
The brief light of our souls—
child too sad to show its face—
shone upon my life, revealing
all the things I'd done
that can and will be used
as evidence against me.

The Waiting Room

No one looks at anyone else.
No one speaks: we are sick.
We slouch, careful not to touch
one another, turning the pages
of magazines, pretending to read.
A man comes in but there are no chairs,
so he stands against the wall.
He looks out the window
wondering what disease
is buried in his body
like a treasure.
If life is a miracle,
then death is, too.
I look out the window.
The woman next to me
looks out the window.
Late winter afternoon.
Darkness coming down.
A nurse turns on another lamp,
keeping the room bright.
But the examining room is dark
as the doctor's eyes, hidden
behind the strongly focused beam
shooting out from the silver circle,
his face drawing nearer
to the sick one, light coming
out the center of his head.

Love for the Bottle

The house seems empty without you.
I let the dirty clothes pile up
soberly in the kitchen
and sit like a Puritan
in a straight-backed chair.
I don't know what to do
with my body, the way it wants
to carry me into the future
like a souvenir. I can't go
anywhere, I can't sleep,
but I take off my clothes anyway,
add them to the mound,
this little burial ground
called my past life.
A ten-day affair with reality.
Cleaning house at midnight,
I put things away,
a lover learning to live
alone again, but still dreaming
of the way only she could soothe me,
her body cold as glass.

The Broken Bowl

The broken bowl on the table
looks like two hands, gesturing,
trying to make itself understood.
I believe it wants to tell me
something about sorrow,
and sadness that cannot be overcome.
I lift the two halves
and hold them together
as if I were holding the dead body
of someone I loved.
I touch the broken edges gently
with a white glue that looks like semen.
Now the bowl must learn again
to love itself, to acknowledge
the delicate place where it has broken
in half, to concentrate on what
cannot be forgotten or overcome.
For it is true:
this scar it will carry
into its second life.
The dark vein will always remain.
The bowl on the table has been broken
and will never be the same.

The Decoy

With his knife
he shapes the body,
turning the wood
gently in his hands.
Sanding it smooth,
he burns feathers
down the back,
paints the bird,
digs out a place
for the glass eyes.
Then he drops a pebble
into the hollow body.
My father could set it
adrift in the bay,
bringing birds down
for men to kill.
Instead, he places it
on the hearth
for his grandchild,
a decoy anyone can lift
and admire, something
he has made
that all agree is lovely,
could almost fly away.

The Hearing Aid

My mother — half-deaf,
a small metal box
pinned to her blouse,

and beneath the gray locks
the hidden earphone,
the wire running across

her heart to its home
in her ear — can barely
hear me anymore. I'm

just someone's voice
lost years ago, trying now
to make myself clear,

deliberately now,
so she will see how
hard the words come.

Bent to her breast, I speak
to the heart, almost hopeless,
where hardly anyone

is ever heard.

Portrait of My Father and His Grandson

Because I love my father,
I can see him turning away
from the river and the divers
and the policemen and the red lights;
I can see him walking back
to the house, follow him
down the long hallway
to the child's room;
I can see him bending over
the empty bed and lifting
the heavy white spread
and carrying it back
to the river's edge
to wrap around his grandson.
But even though I love them both,
I cannot see why this should happen,
or tell you what the boy saw
under the water, or how my father felt
standing by the river when the divers came up,
or where he found the strength to survive
that night, hugging the wet body,
wrapping it up against the cold,
carrying it through the darkness,
home.

Apology to Andrew

Last night, I heard your mother,
my sister, crying in her sleep.
She was sleeping with my mother,
who is deaf, and did not wake
to comfort her. Mother and daughter
sleeping in one bed,
trying to make the world whole again.
My mother was there
to make losing you less
painful. But it is
painful. All day
they both had cried,
praying for strength.
I remember saying,
as though it would help,
as though it were true,
there is nothing we can do
to bring him back.
Now strength and rest will come
from what we suffer.
I even made a little metaphor,
stolen from the Bible:
the sun will rise from the darkness.
But last night, dreaming of you
lost in the river, your mother
kept crying,
your grandmother kept sleeping,
and I kept lying
there in the dark

as if I were you,
the dead child,
unable or unwilling to hear.
Andrew, I am sorry:
I always believed in words,
and sent them instead of my body
to comfort the ones I love,
your mother and grandmother,
my sister and mother,
and Andrew, I did not rise
to put my arms around them.

Leaving Town after the Funeral

After the people and the flowers
have gone, and before the stone
has been removed from your mother's house
and carved into a cross, I come back
on my way out of town
to visit your grave. And nothing
is there — only the ground,
roughed up a little, waiting for rain.
I sit down beside you
in my dark glasses
and put my hand on the earth
above your dead heart.
Two workmen are mowing grass
around the graves beside us.
They pretend not to see
I am crying. Quietly,
they walk over to their truck
to give me time.
The day is hot. They hold paper cups
under the watercooler on the flatbed
and drink together.
They are used to this.
The heat. The grief.
After a few minutes the younger one
walks back to work.
He gets down on his knees
and blows cut grass off a stone.
I believe he wants me to know
he will take care of you.

But hard as it is,
I know the truth:
when you drowned, your body
sank into the river forever.
Ten minutes to eight.
Darkness came down quickly.
And now it will be night
for a long, long time.
The workman gets up and goes on
with his work. I get up
and walk back to the car.
Andrew, we know the truth:
the cold child in the casket
is not the one I loved.

For My Sister

Because it was Christmas,
she planted a plastic tree
at the foot of the grave.
She asked her little boy
if he was being good,
then waited for him
to answer. After a moment
she smiled,
and laid wrapped packages
on the cold ground.
These things she did
for herself. She knew
he couldn't hear—
he had the secret now,
attending to
the whispered words
and the gentle sobbing
that was becoming
a kind of music inside her.

Moving Day

Tomorrow our future begins, our lives
already defined by simple things
scattered on the lawn in sunlight.
Carrying small and useless
objects to the car,
we dismantle our house
piece by piece,
brushing the dust of the past,
lifting each moment into the light.
You with the broken teapot,
I with the broken chair,
we bring all the old things with us
to begin our new life.
Back in the rooms we loved,
there's less and less of us to find.
We see only the space we wasted.
I look out the window and count
boxes waiting for the truck.
You see the room now
as it always could have been,
a vase of cornflowers and us.

Passion

A man casts the wide arc
of his passion, looking for something
to believe in again. And again
and again he is disappointed.
Eventually, his passion dies.
He begins to live
in the old way, as if she were still there—
work in the morning, afternoon in the garden—
but alone and without the old urgency.
Evenings he sits on the porch.
For the first time he has begun
to notice his neighbors—
the widow next door,
fathers coming home from the office,
the beautiful children.
He feels himself falling more and more
in love with these people,
no longer strangers to him,
and every evening,
he consciously breathes in the last
of the dying light, the passion
that will stay with him the rest of his life.

A Beginning

Today I am walking in woods
where men with chain saws
are felling trees and other men
with guns are killing deer.
Today I have nothing to praise
and nothing to feel sorry for.
Today I refuse to make the sky
tender or the earth heroic.
Today I will not condemn the trail
leading to the garbage dump
or lose myself in the leaves' fiery colors.
Today I won't pretend to understand
the ways we care for one another.
Today I will simply stand
in these thick woods and love
how the branches of one tree
reach into the branches of another.

At Last We Enter Paradise

❧

The Shadow

Tonight we give up the idea
of night, and now,

darkness,
what shall we do with you?

With light,
who is extinguished?

Everyone, everyone.

All but the shadow, the voice
thrown down in the dirt to burn.

PART ONE

The Abandoned House

Glass cracks underfoot,
dust lifts into light,
flowered wallpaper
blooms and fades,
and everywhere the sad
sweet smell of urine.
The broken stairs,
a test of faith,
ascend to a window
composing the world—
dirt road, valley,
village in the distance,
and, on a far hill,
a small, white,
freshly painted,
empty wooden church.

The Dead Calf

Snow has fallen,
and a mournful lowing
drifts through a slate-gray mist,

bringing the farmer
puttering into clarity
with his son on a slow blue tractor.

The machine idles
as the boy jumps down
and strikes the cow with a stick,

whipping her
to the edge of the field,
where she calls across the pasture

as her heavy calf is carted away
in the baling arms of the tractor.

Grief, 1942

after the photograph by Dmitri Baltermants

In Crimea at the end of winter,
an old woman trudges through mud,
searching among the dead
for her son
while soldiers stand guard.

In her long black coat,
she approaches a corpse,
cries out,
bends down,
opens her arms,
but does not find,
here among so many others,
her son in this body,

this body she gave birth to
and named.

Twelve-Year-Old Drunk

Singing, he staggers
down my street, a half-
empty pint in hand.
Whiskey whirls him
as if he were dancing
in crazy wild circles,
falling down laughing
to wait for the world
to stop spinning.
But he's not laughing,
and the world keeps spinning.
He lies on my lawn like a little old man,
everything suddenly sad.
Even the stars look sick to him.

Girl with Skateboard

She dries herself with a frayed white towel
before the window in her hospital room,
tempting the world with her boyish body,
though the world will never have her.

Down in the park, tiny people
remind her of germs.
Her mother can't come until evening.
Today, everything's making her blue —

friends who say *each day is special,*
the get-well flowers and the slowly dying
heart-shaped helium balloons,
even her purple skateboard, propped in the corner like a gun.

She ties a kerchief
on her head like a pirate
and climbs into bed with her teen magazines,
pictures of boys she'd like to kiss.

Her hand caresses the bud of her breast;
two fingers slip between her legs where she's wet.
She closes her eyes to dream of men
who could have loved her in life,

where all she's known is the rush of skating
in traffic up one-way streets,
drivers honking and cursing
as she passed them in the wrong direction.

Desire

Knowing our desire for details,
the evening news tells us
how the man died, and even a little
of how he lived, his work, and whom he loved.

He worked in an office downtown.
At night he rode the train home.
There's the point of entry: the broken window.
There, the bed where he was sleeping

when he heard the intruder. Now
the camera hurries through the house,
like a reader skimming pages,
to the room where his life

is outlined in chalk
and the knife is held up to the lights.

The Wedding Party

In the clear April sky
over the wedding party
gathered on the beach,
the drunken best man
was flying his Cessna.

He was doing tricks—
loops and rolls—
buzzing the beach
above the beautiful
barefoot bride and groom.

But a single-engine Cessna
is a small plane, its power
limited.
When the best man aimed it skyward
into the curve of a high chandelle,
at the top of the arc
the engine stalled—

and the best man fell to earth
and the newlyweds ran toward the fire.

The Lullaby

When she had the abortion
she didn't tell me.

She took a taxi to the clinic,
signed her name,

and waited with the other women
and one young girl who was sobbing.

That night she told me
she was tired.

She went to bed early
and turned on the fan—

its music helped her sleep—
and through its blades she heard me

singing
as I washed and put away the dishes.

The Loft

I lay on her bed
while she opened windows
so we could see the river
and the factories beyond.
Afternoon light falling
beautifully into the room,
she burned candles,
incense, talking quietly
as I listened—
I, who conspired
to make this happen,
weaving a web of words that held
this moment at its center.
What could I say now?
That I am a man
empty of desire?
She stood beside the bed,
looking down at me
as if she were dreaming,
as if I were a dream,
as if she too had come
to the final shore of longing.
I lay, calm as a lake
reflecting the nothingness
of late summer sky.
Then she spoke—
she said my name—
and I, who did not love her,
opened my arms.

The Visit

My ex-wife blushed and unbuttoned her blouse,
revealing her breasts, the puckered nipples,
and, what I most wanted to see and taste,
the miraculous thin white stream of milk
sputtering and shooting into the air.
Her white shirt open and loose like curtains,
she lifted her baby, offering her breast,
blind nipple in the V of her fingers;
and the child, quiet now, sucking, drinking,
held onto her breast with his greedy hands
until he fell asleep there, sinking deep
into the pure clear dark of infant sleep.
Then I held the baby and tried not to think,
while she buttoned her shirt and fixed us drinks.

The Amputee

My brother-in-law is a doctor.
He cuts off people's legs.
Yesterday at dinner,
between the chicken and the lemon pie,
the phone rang. I heard him
tell the resident,
"You *have* to cut it off."
The resident was young;
he didn't want to do it.
Like my brother-in-law,
I'm older, more experienced.
I've been cutting off
parts of myself for years now
to save my life.

The Examination

"After work, I begin with gin,"
I tell my new doctor,
"three martinis, very dry,
straight up, with olives,
which I drink while preparing dinner.
I live alone,
but set a table —
white cloth, two candles, music,
a bottle of dry red wine
to accompany the meal.
Then I read or watch TV,
sipping beer until I'm sleepy,
sleepy enough to shuffle off
to bed with a snifter of cognac."

While the doctor takes notes,
I think
of Poe. *He drinks,*
wrote Baudelaire,
with speed and dispatch,
as if trying to kill
something inside him,
some worm that will not die....

The doctor says,
"Stop."

The fool wouldn't let me leave
until I swore an oath,
lifting my hand as though making a toast—

to the souls of my unborn children.

After Making Love, I Tell a Ghost Story

Years ago
in this room
where we sleep,
a boy was shot
in a quarrel
over money.
His mother
closed her eyes
and fell over the body,
crying *Lord, Lord,*
as if God might take the bullet back.

Sometimes at night
you can hear her grief,
the grief that haunts this room.
Listen: what we hear
when we make love
is the old woman crying.
She is the terrible muse
who sings us to sleep each night,
the one who watched grief's seed,
the bullet,
blossom in this room,
peopled now

only with darkness,
and tears,
and death,
and us.

Blackout

Our last night together,
a summer storm struck
and the house went dark.
When the sky cleared
and the stars came back,
we sat on the high balcony,
drinking wine, talking in German
about Berlin and Barcelona,
remembering our tiny bed in Paris
and the sleepless nights.

When it was time to say good-bye,
we grew quiet.
Inside the dark house
you lit a candle
and asked me in English
to follow,
the woman I loved
lighting my way,
leading me down the stairs,
and unlocking the door to the dark.

Faith

How can I tell you all the things
I regret? How can I tell you
I never loved enough? How can I
speak of shame, never having spoken
of it before? And in what voice
should I speak, and how should I approach you—
with my shoulders back, as though I am proud
of who I am, proud that I am
now human enough to confess? If I am

to speak to you, it must be
in a low voice—you will have to lean forward
to hear me; my breath will touch you,
lightly, on your cheek. And your breath, too,
will touch me, like the thinking of a god
who never speaks, but is listening.

Things

I go to a dimly lit secondhand store
to lift empty champagne glasses
and open dusty drawers.
I buy the broken chair
and dedicate myself
to its new life.
I leave with the chipped vase,
the cracked violin, the yellowed lace.

I go to bright department stores
where aisles of merchandise
sing their songs
beneath fluorescent lights—
desks, sofas, picture frames,
asking for a reason to exist,
demanding our secrets, our love,
every thing demanding
everything of my life.

The Lake

Each day like a water jug—
filled, emptied, refilled.
I take off my clothes
and walk across the meadow.
So much that is impossible to resolve.
The path is uneven,
my body sways like a woman's.
When I reach the lake,
green and deep and cold,
I stand by the water for a long time
before diving in.

Today I Saw My Child

Today I saw my child
floating down over the lake,
shimmering in the light,
coming down to rest on the water.
As she drifted toward me,
I saw she was the burst seed
of a dandelion,
the soft stuff of a weed.
She floated on the water,
the green water;
my daughter floated on the water.
I thought I heard her singing,
though it may have been
the light, or the breeze,
or the silent sound the water makes
when it translates for the child,
saying, "Look, Father, I am everywhere.
You can touch me.
I am not lost."

White Towels

I have been studying the difference
between solitude and loneliness,
telling the story of my life
to the clean white towels taken warm from the dryer.
I carry them through the house
as though they were my children
asleep in my arms.

The Impossible

for my nephew, 1978–1984

We could be together now,
years later,
sitting on my tattered sofa,
you with your root beer,
me with my bourbon,
watching TV as I explain
the beautiful art of baseball.
Bottom of the eleventh:
the Cubs came back
with three in the ninth to tie
and now the impossible
happens—a rookie,
just up from the minors,
pinch-hits and wins the game.
I am trying to tell
the significance of this.
You snuggle under my arm
and listen,
looking first at me,
then at the television.
But you are still young
and don't understand
though you know enough of love
to look at me
and tell me that you do.

Prayer

When I go to bed
I think how far away I am
from the people I love.
I live in a farmhouse
in the middle of a field
bounded by woods
at the foot of the mountains
in Virginia. From my window
I watch cows slowly cross the pasture.
My ex-wife lives in Boston.
My father and mother live by the sea.
My sister lives by a river.
She stands in the kitchen
and looks out and sees
her living son climbing the tree,
her dead son walking on water.

The Helicopter Pilot

His face is ghoulish
in the green and blue lights
of the cockpit's gauges.
Hovering, he shines

a light on the river,
then slowly descends;
the water backs away
in ever-widening circles.

When people gather
by the water's edge
around a boy's body
laid on a blanket,

his job is done.
He turns his light off
and the sound—
like a scythe—

fades into the night.

The Mother's Song

after Georg Trakl

It was evening.

We were playing together under a tree.
You were curled inside
an old tire tied by a heavy rope
to a high branch.
I was swinging you,
catching you now and then
to cover your face with kisses,
each kiss like a wish
dropping into a deep blue well.
Mother and child. It was enough
just to look at each other
in the cool autumn dusk
as a purple sweetness
settled down from the stars.

I left you only for a moment.
You walked down the stone steps
toward the river,
a blue smile on your face,
and in the calm of your few small years
you died.

That night I stood in the garden
as moonlight poured over flowers and leaves

a silver, inconsolable grief.
I wanted to call your name
but you were a bouquet
in my heart being torn to pieces.

And now, at the hour
when the sun is purple
and a white heron wades in the water,
you appear,
quietly.

Taking my hand,
you lead me under the elms
by the river.
We drop blue petals into the water
while the shadows darken and widen and become one.

The Gift

Because we see the grave
is the size of a door

we would go with him.
But the ground is open

only to one
and love thrown down

in the earth is lost
forever. Now

loving one another
is all we have left.

But who among us
is strong enough

to carry the terrible
gift he has given?

The Color of Grief

We drop petals
on the water
in his memory,

as if he
and the river
were one.

We talk
about him
while the flowers float away.

How lucky we are
he died
in the river behind our house,

where the ducks he loved
waddle up the lawn.
How much better

to remember him here,
where the river whispers
he's alive!

than at the grave,
where his five years
are carved in stone,

and the hardened earth
is silent,
and grief is green

and always edged
with dying flowers;
for we know grief

is blue, like the river,
which takes our flowers
when they are fresh

and carries them away.

Andrew

This is the way I remember my nephew:
at the children's museum in Boston,
sculpting something strange from clay
he said was his mother and Rusty, his dog,
connecting electrical wires
to switch on red revolving lights,
climbing the small fireman's ladder
through hanging sheets of red cellophane
to the window of the tiny house,
like a hero.

At the hotel pool
I taught him to dive.
I called him Superman
when he bravely belly flopped,
then held his body on top of the water
while he kicked across the shallow end.
Thomas, his brother, jumped off the board
making a goofy face. Kate looked up from her book
and laughed, the way she'd laugh later
when she showered with Andrew
and he kissed her on the fanny.

And I remember, when we got home
he picked flowers for his mother—
snapped the blooms off
the neighbor's prize roses,
threw away the thorny stems,
and offered her only blossoms
in his cupped, dirty hands.

At Last We Enter Paradise
95

The Oriental Carpet

Nights like this when I can't sleep
my dog stays with me,
curled on the worn Oriental carpet
I bought at a yard sale
the day the truck hit the lost dog,
a dog that could have been her sister,
they looked that much alike.

It was evening. Summer.
The truck kept going.
I dimmed the lights,
stepped from my car
and knelt down in the road
next to the dog.
She lay still,
blood oozing
from her mouth and anus.
Someone brought a blanket.
The dog looked up at me.
A man stood over us,
shaking his head.
A woman came out of her house,
backed up her station wagon,
and opened the rear door.
We lifted the dog
onto the blanket,
into the car.
Then I drove away,
the red carpet slumped

like a body in the backseat.
Halfway home I noticed
my emergency lights
still flashing—
two green arrows
on the dashboard,
pointing in opposite directions,
beating furiously.

Now my dog's sitting before me,
staring into my eyes.
She'll walk in a circle on the carpet
and then come back.
When it's this late
all she wants for us
is sleep,
to lie down like dogs
on the Oriental carpet,
close our eyes,
let go of our bodies,
and die a little,
yes, die a little.

PART TWO

Back Then

Back then I was broke,
so I painted houses
in the neighborhood
during the day
and worked nights
downtown in a warehouse,
lifting crates of beans
and sacks of rice till dawn.
I preferred painting houses —
working high on a ladder,
alone in the light, my face
speckled with paint —
to the dreary graveyard shift,
the dirt and concrete,
the dim fluorescent lights
and endless droning of forklifts.
But I made good money
those nights in the warehouse
hauling crates to the docks,
loading the trucks and learning
the difficult camaraderie of men;
or learning to fight,
if that's what they wanted,
as two of us fought one night,
driving our forklifts into each other.
He was the quick-tempered foreman
who once held his knife to my throat.
He had the long fingers of a concert pianist
and the strength of any five of us,

but owned no home
and slept in back of the dark warehouse
between walls of cardboard boxes.
I wanted to kill the son of a bitch.
And he wanted to kill me,
but after we fought
he shook my hand
and stole melons from the freezer,
which we ate as the trucks pulled out
and the clean light came
to wash away the night.

Back then I'd come home
at dawn and drink beer,
telling my father about the night shift
while he shaved and dressed for work,
and after he was gone I'd sleep a little
on the damp and twisted sheets,
white curtains bright at the window
in the attic of my parents' house.
I remember those mornings—
going down to the kitchen
where my mother ironed and cooked.
She worked with great seriousness
in the everyday world of the house,
stopping for coffee and a cigarette
to stare out the window
a few minutes in silence.
I never asked
what she was thinking,
but her loneliness
made me think of my father,

a salesman for Dominion Tobacco.
I wondered if she imagined him
as I still did—the young pilot
flying secret missions
over the bamboo jungles of China,
his mask with the rubber air hose
dangling from his face like an elephant's trunk.
As a boy I feared my father flew
with a cargo of bullets and bombs.
But when I was older I learned
my father flew supplies—
crates of food like the ones I loaded
on trucks each night at the warehouse.

As my mother went back to work,
I'd finish my coffee and bread,
kiss her good-bye,
and enter the cool summer morning.
I'd climb to the highest eaves
of the house that took all summer to paint.
I'd drift through the hours,
clearing away cobwebs
or burning wasps' nests,
washing away pigeon shit
or scraping peeling paint
until the wood was smooth.
Then I painted the old house red
with one ten-dollar horsehair brush
and twenty-five buckets of paint.

There was never any money
for me in painting houses.

To make a living you've got to work fast.
Along the edges where white met red,
I'd hang on the ladder for hours
trying to make the lines run true.
But when the house looked good,
people admired the work.
And sometimes I'd look down and see
my father bringing something to eat.
He'd call to me, forty feet up,
Be careful!
then stand and watch me working.
My father understood
the danger of painting tall houses —
his brother fell
and broke his neck.
But I never fell.
I'd finish working
where I was on the ladder,
paint my brush dry
and climb down to join him.
We'd sit in the grass
and eat our sandwiches,
gardens blooming
like paradise around us —
my father and me
talking about work
and what we would do
someday with our lives.

Craziness

The faces of people I've never seen,
a black dog,
a bleak blue hill with bare trees
that could be mistaken for unpeopled crosses —
these are the subjects of my paintings.
My style is primitive;
my method, physical.
I stand on the canvas and fling paint from two brushes,
swirling my arms in crazy wild circles
and leaping back and forth all night
above a canvas that resembles childhood's empty sky.
I love my paintings
but throw them away,
still wet in the morning.
Now that it's dark, I'll paint my body blue
and sleep on the canvas.
When I wake I'll nail the piece to the wall
and call it *Richard,*
Dreaming.
Perhaps by now you have guessed
I am not in love
and live alone.
But don't mistake me for a painter:
I'm a professor of English.
In a drawer I keep my early, unfinished poems.
They could have been written by anyone
but me.
Perhaps I should complete
that bastard of a last chapter

of my dissertation,
Poetry and Becoming
in the Early Unknown Work
of Another American Poet.
The title is impressive,
but my theme of the spirit coming to life
and looking for its voice
is difficult
and resists me.
Perhaps I should surrender
to a more mystical process, the way
spirit loves words into being, the way
I would love you
if you broke down the basement door
to find me sleeping
with brushes and knives
and unfinished manuscripts.
All I ask
is that you be
a compassionate critic
and bring me a cup of coffee.
Listen to me,
you Rationalists, you Naturalists, you Neoclassicists.
Écoutez:
Répétez la phrase:
Je suis Victor Hugo
passed out on the basement floor.
Now that you've awakened me
be kind:
help me up.
Walk with me.
Mornings like this, I like to go out

and walk down the alley
with the garbagemen.
It is healthy to know the physical weight
of things we throw away,
goods touched by who knows how many hands,
and now touched by your hands,
by the gloved hands of the garbagemen,
and by my hands,
naked
and unprofessional.
That's why I listen
for the truck rumbling up the alley
and open the back gate and help the men
throw trash into the big truck's belly.
A garbage truck, like a poet,
welcomes everything—
broken windows, chicken bones, old poems,
uneaten pills, empty metal buckets, a child's glove,
even these painted pictures of imagined people,
this portrait of a black dog,
this bleak hillside with bare blue trees
one might mistake for crosses.

Wild Guesses

I retreated from the world
to the cottage on the cliff,
wanting to live
like a hermit again,
to lose myself in the fog.
Those gray days of mist and rain
I was happy, content
until the wind cleared the fog
and the snowcapped mountain
across the bay
appeared like the god
of another country.

It was, I think, a Tuesday morning.
I stood at the kitchen window
doing dishes. All week
at that window, I'd witnessed
miracles—deer nibbling
the bushes, the blossoming flower
whose name no one knew,
the swift rolling rivers of mist.
Another morning, another oracle
telling me about my life.
Mist signified the thinking
that confused me. The deer stood
for tenderness. The blossoming
was everything beyond the six letters
of beauty. Was I wrong to want
the mountain to mean

something grand and symbolic?
The Indians named the mountain
Koma Kulshan, Great White Watcher,
and went on with their lives.
Now there are no Indians
to teach the language
of understanding.
So I turned away from the window

and turned on my typewriter
and read Keats, now
a decade younger than I.
I read Rimbaud, even younger.
I slipped Mozart, the prodigy,
into the boom box
and went outside.
It was drizzling.
I pulled dry logs
from the damp woodpile
and carried them in to the stove.
I took my morning's sip of bourbon
and ate a piece of bread.
The dishwater bubbled and popped;
grease floated on the surface;
the sonata filled the room.
I put a match to the gas
under the pot of cold coffee
and wrote you a letter
composed of wild guesses
on the meaning of mountains
while the fire blazed
and the house puffed out messages
a hundred years old.

At Last We Enter Paradise

Athens Airport

I never made it to Athens —
a bomb scare in Madrid
grounded the plane
and everyone was evacuated.
I waited in a bar with two Swedes
who insisted on buying me drinks
while soldiers searched our suitcases
with dogs and machines.
When the loudspeaker told us
in seven different languages
the plane was secure
and would soon take off,
the still-sober Swedes
ordered another round,
but I was already bombed
on fear and *cerveza*.
I leaned against the bar's tinted windows
and watched my plane lift off,
its three white lights disappearing
into the night with the Swedes
and my rucksack on board.
But I still had my moneybelt and passport.
I still hadn't seen the Alhambra
or the Costa del Sol. I hadn't been to Africa.
The next day I bought a second-class train ticket south
and three bottles of wine.
I shared a compartment with four teenage girls
who giggled when I lifted a bottle and said, "*Por favor?*"
But I was happy riding with these dark-haired angels

The Blessing
110

and felt no desire to tell them about my wandering life,
where I was going, or how all my things were lost
and spinning in circles in the airport in Athens.

Certain People

My father lives by the ocean
and drinks his morning coffee
in the full sun on his deck,
speaking to anyone
who walks by on the beach.
Afternoons he works
part-time at the golf course,
sailing the fairways like a sea captain
in a white golf cart.
My father must talk
to a hundred people a day,
yet we haven't spoken in weeks.
As I grow older, we hardly talk at all.
I wonder,
if I were a tourist on the beach
or a golfer lost in the woods
meeting him for the first time,
how his hand would feel in mine
as we introduced ourselves,
what we'd say to each other,
if we'd speak or if we'd *talk,*
and if, as sometimes happens
with certain people, I'd feel,
when I looked him in the eye,
I'd known him all my life.

Drinking with My Mother and Father

My mother and father arrive
for their annual visit.
They tell me they love me.
They open a bottle of wine.
"*Salud.* Health."
We spend the day together
under trees, drinking.
My mother gets a little tipsy
and tells a dirty joke.
My father swirls his glass
and tells a long, involved,
convoluted story
that makes no sense at all.
Just like them,
I, too, get a little high
and tell stories all day.
"How wonderful!" we say,
"How wonderful!"

As the sun sets
we stagger off
to a bed of pine needles
on the hill beside my house.
Stones under our heads
softer than pillows,
we watch the sky grow dark.
How quiet we become,
and a little sad,

when the evening sings
and the stars come back,
but even our sadness
has a flavor like wine.

Letter of Recommendation from My Father
to My Future Wife

During the war, I was in China.
Every night we blew the world to hell.
The sky was purple and yellow
like his favorite shirt.

I was in India once
on the Ganges in a tourist boat.
There were soldiers,
some women with parasols.
A dead body floated by
going in the opposite direction.
My son likes this story
and requests it each year at Thanksgiving.

When he was twelve,
there was an accident.
He almost went blind.
For three weeks he lay in the hospital,
his eyes bandaged.
He did not like visitors,
but if they came
he'd silently hold their hand as they talked.

Small attentions
are all he requires.
Tell him you never saw anyone
so adept
at parallel parking.

Still, your life will not be easy.
Just look in the drawer where he keeps his socks.
Nothing matches. And what's the turtle shell
doing there, or the map of the moon,
or the surgeon's plastic model of a take-apart heart?

You must understand—
he doesn't see the world clearly.
Once he screamed, "The woods are on fire!"
when it was only a blue cloud of insects
lifting from the trees.

But he's a good boy.
He likes to kiss
and be kissed.
I remember mornings
he would wake me, stroking my whiskers
and kissing my hand.

He'll tell you—and it's true—
he prefers the green of your eyes
to all the green life
of heaven or earth.

My Painting

In my painting I am flying
in a 1927 Sopwith Camel biplane,
the kind flown in the early war,
with Jesus as my pilot.
We are flying reconnaissance
over a field of wheat
where red cows meditate on the blue
mountains in the distance.
In the bottom right corner,
a circle of children dressed in white
are dancing, celebrating
the eternal life
to come. In the bottom left,
in a purple house, my mother and father
are lying on long wooden tables,
peacefully, surrounded by the glory
of pink geraniums blooming
in heavy clay pots.
When Jesus and I fly past,
the flowered curtains flutter
and the children look up.
Jesus waves good-bye, then
points the plane heavenward,
his eyes raised toward the stars
above the painting. I look
back at the half-finished earth,
at the children and the cows and the house.
There are some last touches I'd like to make,
a little more color, a lake perhaps

with silvery fish leaping
over nets in the water like rainbows.
But Jesus, his eyes on heaven,
doesn't look back, and the plane
is climbing, faster and faster,
and I realize now
he won't turn back
even if I
tried to explain
that I'm not finished with my painting
and my painting is not finished with me.

My Father's Buddha

When I was a boy
and afraid of the dark,
I'd steal downstairs
when everyone was sleeping
and kneel before the old sideboard,
my father's liquor cabinet.
I was learning to drink,
each night turning a key
and opening two small doors
as if this were the beginning
of a long dark book.

One night I discovered something
hidden behind the bottles —
a small wooden statue of the Buddha,
lacquered gold,
inlaid with precious stones,
colored glass, and bits of mirror —
a statue my father stole
during the war from a village
in Burma. The Buddha
was the only thing he took
when the troops looted the temple.

I was thirty-three,
my father's age during the war,
and had finally stopped drinking
when he told me this story

one winter morning over tea.
He unlocked the cabinet
and gave me the statue,
wrapped now, carefully,
in clean white muslin.
He never asked to be forgiven;
he simply lifted it into the light.

Now the Buddha sits on my desk,
compassionless, half-smiling,
mindful as I devote myself
to the task within the gift,
to do as my father taught me:
save one thing
and offer it to the morning sun
which sees all things
for what they are.

The Poet's Heart

Think of the Buddhist monks
who sat in the road
at the start of the war,
saffron robes soaked in gasoline,
and set themselves on fire.

Think of the violence,
the immolation, the composed desire
for peace
silently spoken to ashes;
think of the gift,
the eloquence of their burning.

Poems, too, burn
like a body on fire,
devoted, implacable,
not in flashing epiphany,
but steadily, like the priests
and the world they could imagine.

Think, too, of Shelley's drowned body
burning on the beach in Italy,
of Trelawny, who reached
into the fire
to steal the poet's heart.
The poet's heart:
what the fire could not consume.

The Fence Painter

By the time I wake,
the fence painter is ready
to knock off for the day.
The black lines of the fence
fall away behind him
more evenly, more beautiful
for the touch of his brush.
His forearms black with asphalt paint,
as though part of the brush and bucket,
he concentrates on the unfinished wood
until it matches to his satisfaction
an unblemished darkness he imagines.
"I like to start early," he says,
"before the sun gets too hot."
I can't say whether he's happy,
but I envy the fence painter
the early morning hours
and the peace of hard work,
the way he puts away his tools in the afternoon
and drives home in his truck.

The Abandoned Garden

In late October it rains.
The house grows chill and dank.
Out back, the abandoned garden,
gone to seed beneath the frost,
desolate under a half-moon.

Not yet November,
but already cold enough
to light the stove.
That's good —

long nights before the fire,
reading and drinking tea —

as good as summer days,
my shirt on a nail,
my hands in the dirt.

Thanksgiving

Today I cleaned the gutter's garbage
and raked the lawn's litter of leaves,
then lugged the stuffed green plastic bags
out back behind the garage.

I pulled dead stalks of flowers
and snipped the perennials. I turned the soil
until the dirt fell black and loose
from my shovel, then scraped the beds smooth.

Tired of summer's confusion of growth,
I appreciate winter's order,
the season composed of less and less
until nothing's left
but the outline of the garden's border.

Song of the Old Man

I might have died when I was young,
my body all muscle and desire,
and believed death was beautiful

but then I would have missed
the beauty of the body's
decline, how we fall

away like a flower,
surviving the season
to bloom just once,

throwing sweet scent into the air
and becoming a part of everything there.

A Vision

Last night I found myself
alone on a beach at sunset,
my back to a vast, glittering city.
I was the only witness
to the mountains rising
out of the sea toward heaven.
I thought it was the land of the dead,
but saw no people, not even a tree,
only rock and sand, sickly green
in the waning daylight.
I ran through the streets
back to the high-rise apartment,
took the elevator to the top
to tell my father, my mother,
join me—hurry—
by morning the vision may be gone—
but my parents had been dead for years.
My sister came in from the study,
an open book in her hands,
and calmly asked me,
"Hasn't Andrew taught you anything?"
And then I realized how beautiful it is
to talk with the dead
who appear as mountains
in visions that send you running
back to the living.
I opened the sliding glass door
and stood on the balcony
beneath the empty evening sky

and looked without grief
at the city's million lights
sparkling like heaven,
illuminating the city where people I love
and people I've never met
wait for the quiet moment
when at last we enter paradise.

Boundaries

after Ma Chih-Yuan

If the crow
perched on the dead branch
of the apple tree,
his back to the dark,
sees the sun setting
behind the ridge of pines,
the broken fence where a skinny horse
searches for grass,
the spring brook flowing
between the road and my house,
then he also sees me
opening my door and crossing
the rickety little bridge
that connects me to the world.

A Perfect Time

The Key

This is my key to happiness,
the key to my room
in the Hôtel du Paradis.
The tireless Algerian
keeps the key behind the bar all day
to return to me at midnight
when I climb the narrow, winding stairs
with my pounding heart and loneliness.
The Algerian calls out *bonne nuit;*
I struggle with the broken lock.
A flimsy door, I could kick it down,
but when I am patient,
when, in my quietest voice,
I say *please,*
it opens
and lets me in.
I turn on the light
and there is the cell of my dreary room—
the unmade bed, the open suitcase,
pitcher of stale water on the table.
I unlatch the window
and lean into the night
above torches of countless streetlamps
and wild cars carving the boulevards
with blades of rushing lights.
I pray to the moon
rising above dark steeples,
ask the moon to translate for stars
listening unseen

beyond the city's dazzling lights.
Night after night,
sitting in my window, hungry and tired,
or pacing back and forth before my desk,
I have come to love
the one dim bulb
dangling from the ceiling on a thin black cord.
I have come to trust
the smallest illumination,
the tiniest omen,
wallpaper peeling away
to reveal origins and mysteries,
the hotel's ten thousand ghosts
and the sickly sweet perfume of their bodies.
I've learned to write or read
to the music of motorcycles
roaring down tangled streets
or to fall asleep
long after midnight
to singing on sidewalks below.
Locking my door,
I turn out the light
to the distant wailing of sirens,
sit on my bed and consider my key,
a silver key with a worn yellow tag
the yellow of a dying daffodil,
room number 8 in red,
symbol of infinity
and my lucky number.
I've begun to believe
in the numerology of my birth—
August 8, '53 —

three 8s in a row,
three affirmations
I will live forever.
I put the key under my pillow,
lie down,
cross my arms on my chest
and feel my beating heart
promising everything
if only I can wait until morning
when I wake
to the wild music
of all the city's church bells,
when I open my door
and lock it behind me,
when I bound down the winding stairs
that rush to the street,
to flower shops and cafés,
to the parks and river
and every stranger waiting
to ask my name
and greet me with a kiss —
all this,
my heart promises,
tomorrow,
after I've turned out the light
and slept on the narrow bed,
after I've awakened
and returned the key
to the smiling Algerian,
who waits behind the bar each morning
with my hunk of bread and my coffee,
my sugar and my cream.

A Perfect Time
133

Scars

This hollow of dead skin
the size of a coin
centered on my left shin
was a gift from the ocean—
the sharp blade of a shell
tore my leg open
to show the bone that carries me.
This ragged scar on my arm
I earned being introspective
walking in woods—
rusted barbed wire
ripped through my shirt to awaken me.
And the small white arc?
This tiny moon over my left eye?
—appeared from nowhere one day in the mirror.

My body reveals its history.
I would show you
invisible tokens
of sorrow and joy—
grief-scars and love-scars.
I remember crying all day
when my mother was
dying. I remember
Aunt Ruby, who took me in,
lifted me,
and covered my face with kisses.
I ran to the bathroom

and saw in the mirror
the bee-stings of her lipstick.

When I was a boy
I dreamed I could fly.
It was wonderful to soar
over my mother's house
with its locked doors
and shuttered windows!
Dreaming taught me
the body is nothing,
less than nothing,
less than a dream.

This morning I ate the fish
I caught last night.
I laid the fish on the kitchen counter—
an old, scarred, grandfather fish,
rainbow of flesh pale with age,
scales torn and dangling.
With a knife I cut off the head,
slit open the belly.
With my fingers I removed
brown and green entrails,
the tiny heart. From the sink,
the fish's ancient eye watched
as I ran the knife over the body,
the silver scales leaping in air.
I cooked the fish
in my grandfather's iron skillet,
battered and scratched from the years.
The hot oil smoked; the fish sizzled in the pan.

I love my body in the morning,
hunger raging inside me.
The body's hunger is beautiful.
I fill it with the wisdom of fish.
If I could fly, I'd visit my mother
in heaven. I'd hold her angel-hands
in my scarred mortal hands,
and thank her
for giving me the world.

Lanterns

To believe in love,
I leave my house

before sunrise, my quest
sanctified by blue and gold

lights that burn
in tenement rooms

where a child wakes,
cries,

stirring a woman
who sleepily rises

to the child's hunger,
unbuttoning her nightshirt

and drifting down the hall
past the kitchen, where

beneath the halo
of the fluorescent light,

a man sits, drinking coffee,
waking to the particulars

of his existence —
woman, baby, radiator knocking

the chill from the room
as he bends like one in prayer

to lace his boots,
as he leaves to become

one of many men and women
in dungarees and hardhats

moving forward, inch by inch,
with tractors and earthmovers,

working for weeks, months,
to make a new road,

concentrating,
this day,

on one broken-up square of highway
and the task of making it smooth,

working patiently as monks
in a monastery courtyard,

monks raking pebbles
in ripples and waves

to achieve the semblance
of ever-changing sea,

suggesting the beauty
of everything in nature

blessed,
as all things are,

by the sky,
by ten thousand stars

faintly visible
beyond the lanterns

hanging from branches of cherry trees,
red paper lanterns that burn each evening,

lit sometimes by a novitiate,
sometimes by the master.

The Mystery

It's not easy
now that I live in the city
to find a quiet wooded place
to meditate on death,
to sit in shade
and consider the mystery
that worried me as a child:
where do animals go to die?
When I was a boy I would lie
beneath maples and elms for hours,
studying sky
vanishing
beyond lush branches
rocking back and forth in wind.
When I was a boy
I'd wander hushed woods all day
in search of the blacksnake
coiling into a question mark
one last time
to die... but it's not easy
here in the city's forest preserve
when cyclists race by on concrete paths
through woods into crowded parking lots
where picnickers feast on sandwiches
from trunks of cars in the blazing noon.
Here I'm tempted to forget death
and drink with these noisy families,
to ask for a deviled egg
or a piece of fried chicken

and, in return, quote a line of poetry
among the parked cars and folding tables—
but looking at their faces
I only think of lines that grieve.
If I'm in search of the mystery's answer,
why observe
the pair of kissing lovers
strolling hand in hand from the parking lot
into tall grass on the hill?
Look at them
taking off their clothes
on the bed
of their red-checked blanket,
oiling each other's body
tenderly in the sun.
Lovers know no grief.
Only children
search the woods
for the burial place of deer,
muddy graves of raccoons,
bones of herons hanging in branches,
tortoise shells lodged
in mossy hollows of rotten logs.
I consider these things
as I lie against a willow by the lake
and nap. When I wake, two men in a rowboat
are fishing just offshore, quiet and serious
in the last evening light.
They do not see me. I could be a deer
or fox come down to the water
for one last drink.
It is almost dark. Everyone

is gone. Now wild teenagers
arrive in vans, slamming doors,
parading toward the lake, carrying a box
of loud music that drowns their voices,
carrying their young bodies through darkness
to the lake's black water
where the moon, too,
will extinguish itself before dawn.
I look through the veil of willow branches
at evening's first star.
From this private, hidden place,
this shaded retreat,
the cries of teenagers
baptizing themselves in the forest's lake
grow distant and remote.
I remember when I was little,
afraid of wind in trees at night.
My Aunt Ruby would hold me
and rock me against her breast.
I knew then the simple answer:
animals know
when it is time to die.
They leave their own kind
and wander off
in search of a tranquil place to rest,
a serene wood pierced by a perfect ray of moonlight.

Ice

The iceman—
taciturn, unshaven, his face
weathered and gray—
wore a gray felt hat
with the brim turned down,
a black band of sweat around the crown
dignified
by a small green feather.
I fed sugar cubes to the brown draft horse
that pulled his heavy wagon up our hill
while my aunt fetched her beaded purse.
My aunt had no need of ice:
she owned a Frigidaire.
Ice was a strange and frivolous gift
she bought for me
those long, hot summer afternoons in the South.
The iceman dropped
her quarter in his apron,
pulled on thick, scarred leather gloves,
and jerked down fiercely
on a rusted handle,
cold smoke rushing out the thick black door.
With heavy silver tongs
he dropped a block of burning ice in my hands;
I carried the ice up my aunt's flowered walk
and sat all day in the shade of a tree
just to watch it melt.

Leaning close to the clean-smelling chill,
I stared into the core of frozen water,
my hands cupping its sides,
consulting the crystal,
waiting for the mystery
of my life that summer
to reveal itself, my future
written by the iceman's tongs
in lacy veins that ran to the heart of the ice
and resembled, I realize, the filigrees of frost
on the window I'm looking through now.

2. CLIMBING

Outside — Chicago, January — a woman
hurries down the middle of the street,
head down against wind and snow.
Where is she going
so early on a Sunday morning?
What is she rushing toward?
I drop another ice cube into my glass
and drink to six AM.
Up all night, I read a novel
about mountain climbing in Europe,
the skill it takes to survive
with pitons, hammers, and ropes.
The heroes are two men
who have grown to love each other,
as friends who risk their lives together
sometimes do. I confess
I have never climbed a mountain.

Friends out West tell me
the gentle rounded hills
of the ancient Blue Ridge
aren't really mountains at all:
no looming icy summits,
no dangerous impossible heights.
Once, after my divorce,
I hiked all day with my father
to the highest peak in Virginia.
He dressed that day
as if we were going to dinner —
blue coat, tie, oxfords.
I offered to trade shoes,
and halfway up, sitting on a log, we did.
The trail through the woods
opened onto jagged outcroppings of rock,
a clear autumn afternoon,
trees dying into brilliant colors
throughout the Shenandoah.
We sat on the cliff's edge.
His feet dangled in my tennis shoes;
my feet dangled in his oxfords.
The sky melted into the valley.
When I think of my father,
I think of the mountain
and wearing his slick-soled oxfords.
Walking the trail back down in the dark,
I slipped and he grabbed my hand.
The long hike up
he never complained,
though climbing in oxfords
must have been like climbing a mountain of ice,

like the mountain in the novel
I read all night, imagining
my father and me
on the icy face of a mountain in France,
our lives tied together by ropes.

3. THE WINDOW

This morning
in the first gray light
anyone who cared
could watch the dirty city slowly vanish
dreamlike into a snowstorm,
snow falling
on the tracks of the woman who passed.
Now snow falls
on the memory of her.
I was five the summer
I was sent to live with my aunt
where the draft horse and ice wagon
climbed our gently sloping street,
leaving a trail of water
drying in the sun
—just as my warm hand
leaves a trail of water
as it brushes the icy window clear.

The Black Hat

What should I do with the black hat
of the burglar who tried to break in
today? It was noon. I was in the basement
doing laundry
when he kicked in the back door.
I yelled, "Son of a bitch!"
He took off down the alley—
muscular, tall, younger than I.
For a block I chased him
but gladly lost him in the shadows,
then ran home, breathless,
and with shaking hands called the police.

When my house is burglarized,
they take my Walkman,
cameras, little things
they can carry and sell on the street.
I come home to my walls
ravaged with gang signs,
crowns and crosses
like the ones spray painted in the alley.

"Gang signs
don't mean anything,"
the police said, looking around the house.
"Thieves throw blame on enemies."
What cops want
"is a detailed description—
age, height, race—"

of the man who disappeared down the alley.
To prove the thief's existence,
I introduced as evidence
the black hat
that flew off his head
when he ran.
"Keep it," they said,
"a souvenir,"
tearing their report from the pad.

I'm going to wash the hat,
wear it to work tomorrow.
I'll wear it to keep the sun out of my eyes
mornings when I weed the garden.
In the black hat
I'll look like a carpenter
as I repair the broken door.

Because I don't want to dream
about thieves at night,
I'll wear the black hat
in bed. I'll read Hikmet
and memorize the poem
in which he refuses to wear a hat
until everyone owns a hat.

I'll write a poem called "The Black Hat"
in the form of an epistle
or prayer,
pin my poem to the hat
along with the police report,
and hang the hat

where anyone can steal it—
in the tree branching out
over the alley's crosses and crowns.

"The Black Hat"—
inspired by the man who would rob me,
dedicated to the god
of thieves.

If I Should Die

If I should die this afternoon
who will take care of my dog?
Who will let her out this evening
and walk her twice around the block,
letting her stop now and then to sniff
an especially delicious turd
some other dog has left behind
just for her, a gift
hidden among leaves and tall grass
that she discovers
like a little girl at an Easter egg hunt?
Like a little girl, she needs someone to feed her.
Who will fill her red bowl with the bone-shaped feed
that smells of old socks, her favorite fragrance,
lovely aroma, gourmet that she is?
And who will howl with her at the moon at midnight
in the backyard as I do? Who will get down
on all fours, snarling by the back gate
at ghosts and thieves?
Who will bury his nose in snow or dirt or mud?
Who will walk in circles, curl on the old pillow,
dream the dream of the dog —
as I do, night after night,
lying on my back, my snout and whiskers twitching,
my eyes opening and closing,
my paws trembling, my legs shuttling back and forth?
Dreaming like a dog,
I chase whatever it is I want
but never catch in life,

though, in my dreams, like a dog, I do—
I catch it and bite down hard;
it can't get away;
I'm devouring it now, whatever it is,
whatever it was I wanted
all my life
and begged for
every day
like a dog.

The Remedy

Tonight
I'm cooking tomato soup
in my yellow pot,
asking basil and a dozen cloves of garlic
to cure my pneumonia.

This morning,
appealing to the earth
to nurse me back to health,
appealing to the summer sun hot on my back
to burn away the cold gray clouds
gathered in my lungs,
I shambled to the garden,
filled my wicker basket
with vegetables and herbs,
and slowly, weakly,
pulled weeds
grown wild these long weeks of illness.
I despise weeds
as I despise pneumonia.
I stood among the chrysanthemums in my red robe and dared
weeds or death to mess with me.
I have two hands that aren't afraid to get dirty
and a knife that chops basil and celery.
I have a blender to puree tomatoes.
I know two Spanish onions who weep
over my feeble body,
who are willing to die
that I may live.

All day the soup simmered. All day
I opened cupboards and cabinets,
mixing elixirs, tonics,
relying on secret potions
and herbal concoctions
to cure me of all my diseases —
angelica for ills of my body,
valerian for ills of my mind,
the heart-shaped leaves of the pansy
to heal a broken heart.
To dispel dark thoughts
I rubbed my temples with lavender oil
and smeared crushed mint on my forehead.
I cast spells,
devising words of a vow
not to dwell on the past
or happiness I've known.
Sitting in my father's chair,
plucking honeysuckle flowers
made me remember
innocence
and drinking sweet nectar
drop by drop
made me forget
ruined cities
and my worn leather suitcase
filled with the willow branches
of my bitterness
and the chicory
of my anger.
Following doctor's orders —
while the yellow pot dozed and dreamt on the stove —

I slept in the sunroom all afternoon
like Rimbaud's dead soldier beside the brook,
the bullet hole in his heart like a blossom.
But unlike the soldier,
toward evening
I rose again.

The soup simmers on the stove,
aroma of garlic and basil
perfuming the house.
Like a French chef,
I lift the lid of my yellow pot with a flourish,
dip my spoon,
taste the tomatoes, smack my lips,
add spices—
dill, black pepper, sugar, cilantro—
working by intuition,
adding a little white wine
and a dash of tabasco
to cure the blues
that come with pneumonia.
Tonight there's almost nothing
left of my voice,
and yet it makes me happy,
here in my kitchen,
to sing a song
about the country
and gardens laid out
in tight little squares
like sonnets. It makes me happy
when I devote a verse
to lush gardens

that spring up like hope
on abandoned lots
in dying cities.
Tonight, delirious
with fever and exhaustion,
I stare into the black heart
of the kitchen window vivid with visions
of old men and old women in broad-brimmed hats
opening heaven's rickety garden gate
and walking through the country of air
to bring me gifts —
flowered aprons full of tomatoes.

Seven weeks
the Spanish moss
of pneumonia has hung
in the branches of my lungs;
seven weeks I've been
unable to get out of bed.
But tonight,
in the kitchen in my smelly red robe,
stirring the yellow pot with a wooden spoon,
tonight
I curse infirmity
and celebrate the dignity
of slowly dying gardeners
who each day water onions
or plant flowers for sweethearts.
Like pulling weeds,
it makes me feel good to forgive the wasted
healthy days of my youth,
to know that tomorrow

I'm going to wake and work again,
harvesting what the earth has promised,
daring the weeds, daring death.
I repeat: I've got two hands
unafraid of dirt.
I curse darkness.
I spit on the night that devours me.
I pour my bowl of soup
and recite this poem,
this magic,
this incantation cleaving sickness from
health. I open the door
and carry my bowl to my table in the garden,
blue-white moonlight
dusting my skin like pollen.
In the night-sweet air,
I fold my hands in prayer
and say grace, giving thanks
for tomatoes and herbs,
chrysanthemums and moonlight,
asking to live
a while longer in this body,
this body I bless at every meal,
crossing it with one hand,
feeding it with the other.

The Suit

I am hungry
and have an hour,
so I stop at the corner diner
across from the railroad tracks
alongside Rosewood Cemetery.
I hesitate in the doorway
as a train rolls past
with its litany of empty windows,
wondering if the lunch waitress
is wearing her red hair pulled back
or letting it fall in her eyes.
Inside, I take off my suit coat,
fold it, notice how the lining shines
like silk inside a coffin.
In the red vinyl booth
with the jukebox on the wall,
I flip through songs,
reading titles I'd forgotten,
remembering lyrics
as if they were poetry....
                             The waitress
never looks at me;
tapping her pen on her pad
she asks if I want more time
and waits to write whatever I say.
I order and eat
black bean soup
doused with hot sauce
before asking for the daily special —

turkey and mashed potatoes and carrots,
tossed green salad,
coffee and chocolate pie.
Halfway through dessert,
I retrieve a newspaper
drying on a steaming radiator.
As I sip my coffee,
my friend's obituary
smudges and dirties my hands.
I think of him yesterday —
his closed eyes,
his body dressed in suit and tie
lying among the flowers,
my friend who never wore a suit.
How strange to see
the mystery of his existence
reduced to nothing
but a few words
written by someone who never saw him,
the song of his long life
brief as a poem.
I ask the waitress
                    what time is it?
as I pay the bill.
Writing the total on her little pad,
she says *quarter to two.*
I want her eyes to look into mine
but it's terrifying
to really look at someone
and risk small stars of pain
igniting in their eyes,
though sometimes

looking into eyes can be
just like making love.
I look down.
I look at my suit coat,
shining,
and put it on.
My suit makes me feel
italicized.
March seventeenth. Two o'clock.
I leave the diner
and walk through the tunnel
under the railroad embankment,
wishing a train would fly overhead
like thunder, like wild clouds of glory.
But there is only the long silence of empty tracks.
And on the other side,
a few cars driving slowly through the rainbow archway,
the entrance to Rosewood Cemetery.

The Blacksnake

If only I could make amends
for the blacksnake I killed.

My wife was afraid
of snakes getting into our house
through the pipes.
I was teetering on a ladder,
painting the tallest part of the house,
the gable where a lightning rod stabs the sky,
when I saw the blacksnake flowing
toward the open cellar door.
I climbed down,
ran to the shed for the shovel.
When I returned,
the snake was half-hidden beneath dead leaves
between the house and the flowering forsythia.
Imagine the blacksnake recoiling
before the raised blade—

I buried the snake in the orchard.
That was the last summer
my wife and I lived
in harmony.
The ensuing years brought
poverty,
the death of my nephew,
our divorce. If anyone asked
I'd tell them I still love
the house we lived in,

the way she laughed,
the animals that came down
from the mountains at night.
But it's no good
to talk about the blacksnake.
Nothing I say can change what happened.
I killed it because I loved her.

The Beginning

I'll never forget the night
the phone rang
and my father told me,
"Andrew is dead."
A summer evening in Earlysville....
Sky beginning to purple
over the Blue Ridge....
I was in the living room
dancing
to some music I can never listen to
again.
I was doing the watusi, the skate,
even stranger dances I'd invented
those long evenings
of separation
from my wife, the woman
I was beginning to love at last.
Six clowns hung on the wall—
faces my nephew had painted
and given as a gift,
some smiling, some crying,
one with closed eyes
opening his green lips
to scream.
I had to stop dancing,
lift the needle from the black grooves
circling endlessly,
turn away from the clowns
and walk through the house

past things my wife had left behind.
I walked through the kitchen
and looked out at the mountains,
the beautiful evening,
the world I loved
dying into the dark.
I picked up the phone.
Heard my father's voice.
And closed my eyes,
closed them forever,
though the stars were just beginning
to come toward me —
small bright needles.

Sacrifices

All winter the fire devoured everything—
tear-stained elegies, old letters, diaries, dead flowers.
When April finally arrived,
I opened the woodstove one last time
and shoveled the remains of those long cold nights
into a bucket, ash rising
through shafts of sunlight,
ash swirling in bright, angelic eddies.
I shoveled out the charred end of an oak log,
black and pointed like a pencil;
half-burnt pages
sacrificed
in the making of poems;
old, square handmade nails
liberated from weathered planks
split for kindling.
I buried my hands in the bucket,
found the nails, lifted them,
the phoenix of my right hand
shielded with soot and tar,
my left hand shrouded in soft white ash—
nails in both fists like forged lightning.
I smeared black lines on my face,
drew crosses on my chest with the nails,
raised my arms and stomped my feet,
dancing in honor of spring
and rebirth, dancing
in honor of winter and death.
I hauled the heavy bucket to the garden,

spread ashes over the ground,
asked the earth to be good.
I gave the earth everything
that pulled me through the lonely winter—
oak trees, barns, poems.
I picked up my shovel
and turned hard, gray dirt,
the blade splitting winter
from spring. With hoe and rake,
I cultivated soil,
tilling row after row,
the earth now loose and black.
Tearing seed packets with my teeth,
I sowed spinach with my right hand,
planted petunias with my left.
Lifting clumps of dirt,
I crumbled them in my fists,
loving each dark letter that fell from my fingers.
And when I carried my empty bucket to the lake for water,
a few last ashes rose into spring-morning air,
ash drifting over fields
dew-covered
and lightly dusted green.

My Sister's Garden

She hated going into the garden alone.
The garden, with high grass choking the baby's breath
and weeds crowding the daisies,
had become a recrimination.
She would walk out each morning with her mug of hot coffee,
her heart full of hope,
and the garden — wild, untended, its red and yellow blossoms
lost in tall green shoots of burst seed tendrils —
would be a reminder that yesterday,
and the day before,
and for all the days of spring,
she had done nothing, had forsaken the work
of weeding and watering,
splitting of roots and bulbs,
mulching, the matching of colors —
purple of iris against pink of azalea.
What *had* she done
those long, cool spring afternoons?
What had she done yesterday
when the sun rose and the heat came?
She had lounged in her chair in the garden and waited
for the sun to come around the tree
and bathe her face with light.
She had dreamed of the time
when she'd first entered the yard,
when the garden was only an idea,
something growing in her imagination.
Taking paper, she had drawn plans,
herbaceous borders, banks of flowers,

small hills of camellias,
the far wall covered with honeysuckle and clematis.
She had taken a spade and turned soil,
making an outline, lifting dirt, a curving line
rolling away in a black wave,
the blade of the shovel whispering
each time she leaned the weight of her life
on her boot and pushed down.
And how many days passed
kneeling in dirt with marigold seeds, daffodil bulbs,
small pots of perennials she'd bought at the garden store?
... Now, flowers come up year after year,
bloom in spite of her.
Bulbs open
and the green tongues of their longing kiss the air,
buds opening
in the sun like memory,
a memory of pain
she bows to and smells like a flower
whose fragrance stays for days,
memory
the garden she may enter at any moment
simply by opening her door and stepping outside
to lose herself
in the world growing wild around her,
the world with all its blossoming and perfumes,
its dazzling light and dew, the world
that is ten thousand worlds—
small plateaus of leaves,
the rope of each stem,
the dusty cloud of every petal—
a beautiful web in which she, now,

has become only the smallest part
and the only part
that knows and feels and believes
in pain, but also knows
she, too, must
blossom.

Listening

It was all I could give—
my eyes two drops of rain,
my hands on the table two sleeping birds,
my chest turned toward you with no shield,
the two wounds of my ears,
my slow-breathing silence,
my head slowly nodding
a flower heavy with dew,
the sun coming from behind a cloud,
a piece of light
falling on the table between us like bread,
falling on hands, our hands touching,
this moment of my listening,
this dark time of your voice, saying,
"this flower, this light, this bread,"
your words a piece of bread
you break in two
and share.

Leaving Los Angeles at Last

I'm stealing my friend's Volkswagen,
pushing it out of his driveway while he's sleeping,
rolling it down the hill toward Silver Lake
to get the beat-up old beauty started.
Mine is a long, dangerous journey
requiring a stolen car, an assumed name,
the mind of a thief, and the heart of a sinner.
I'm saying good-bye to Los Angeles at last,
to movie stars and La Casa Bonita,
to the *Times* and Hare Krishnas.
I'm ripping the suit off my back
as if it were in flames
and throwing my shoes out the window —
two dead birds on the side of the road.
I'm flying down the Hollywood to the Santa Monica,
the 405 to San Diego,
smuggling what I need to survive
in Bibles hollowed out with a razor —
tapes of Bach and Miles Davis,
photographs of my beautiful childhood
and photographs of the agony
of my youth and first loves.
I'm hanging a ribbon of thorns
from the rearview mirror,
turning up the radio
and singing "Unchain My Heart,"
improvising, changing the words, making the song
an anthem for martyrs and saints.
After crossing the border

I'll travel by night,
sleeping by day on the empty beach
or in caves in the mountains above the desert.
So no one will suspect me,
I'll wear a serape like the old Robert Bly,
a white linen suit like Faulkner.
I'll master the art of disguise,
walk with a limp,
speak with an odd, hard-to-place accent—
could be French, could be Romanian.
In the small villages,
with my sunglasses and zinc oxide,
my Bermudas, straw hat, and camera,
I'll look like a Swedish tourist.
I'll abandon the Volkswagen
and slip through Mexico and Honduras,
be tempted by Belize,
but will lose myself for good
in Ecuador or Uruguay.
I'll take a room above a quiet *taberna*
and lie in bed all day, remembering.
The doors of my balcony will be open
to let in dreams or memories,
the curtains—if there are curtains—blowing
in the breeze from the ceiling fan.
And perhaps, in Paraguay or Peru,
I'll be forgiven. I'll enter
the little white adobe church,
the one with the painted wooden Madonna
grieving in her green and yellow gown,
silver-blue drops of paint on her cheeks.
Kneeling at the altar,

light pouring through open windows like grace,
I'll bow before the priest,
kiss the hem of his robe,
kiss his bare ankles and feet.
Finally I'll begin to weep,
knowing at last the hungry flames
of the candles have devoured
whatever dream was meant for me.
Beyond prayer, beyond blessing,
there will be nothing
for the priest to do
but bow his head and watch me cry,
laying his hand on my shoulder
as if I were his long-lost son
and he my father.

The Novel

I.

For two days I've been crying,
from Paris to Rome, from Rome to Palermo,
weeping and sobbing here on the train
over a nineteenth-century novel.
Some paragraphs are so beautiful
I lean my head against the window
while villages fly past
like books I'll never open.
When I come to the last few sentences
of an exquisitely painful chapter,
I drop the novel in my lap
or crush it to my chest
and cover my face with my hands,
trembling and shaking.

People on the train
don't know what to do with me
or why I rock back and forth
clutching my book and sniffling.
From Paris to Rome,
the French hated me for crying.
They blew smoke in my face
and cursed me in their beautiful language.
But now, along the Amalfi Coast,
beside blue waters and grottoes,
the great hearts of the Italians
take pity —
they offer me water,

offer me wine.
We open the window and smoke together
until I compose myself.
These are my five angels —
a baker from Napoli,
a nun,
young Rafael the fisherman,
and an old married couple,
young lovers once,
now shrunk to the size of children.
The baker from Napoli speaks for them all,
asking what troubles me.
The five Italians lean forward.
For a long moment I'm silent,
looking down at the novel
that is the story of my life,
a secret between the author and me.
I am the hero,
and though I am brave,
indefatigable, loyal, intrepid,
I cannot bear to hear it all again.
My story is blessed with moments of joy,
but they are brief
and flicker like distant stars.
The author knows
truth is tragic.
Relentless, tireless, devoid of sympathy,
he talks and talks
like the heartbeat of time
while I grow weaker and weaker,
no longer a hero,
but a boy again,

weeping when my mother falls ill in the castle,
weeping when Fabiana, my little sister,
is abducted by thieves and gypsies
and forced to dance naked
before a fire in the camp of the hussars.

The Italians are waiting.
I look up at the luggage rack,
suitcases and plastic bags
piled precariously over their heads.
I look out the window at blue doors and green doors
of whitewashed houses built on the edges of cliffs
here at the foot of the famous volcano.
When I finally lean forward, I whisper,
slowly, so they will understand,
"My wife died,
and my child,
horribly,
in an accident,
in America, America,
an accident in America,
my wife and child,
morto, morto."
The Italians lean back,
overcome, delighted,
crossing themselves,
everyone talking at once.
My confession makes them happy,
makes them hungry.
They bring out sandwiches,
pears, olives, and cheese.
We feast all afternoon

until sated and sleepy,
until they all lean back in their worn red seats
and the baker, with his hands, asks,
"And now?"
I tell them I'll retreat
to an island to rest,
recover, renew my life
again. I tell this
in broken Italian
and simple French,
using only the present tense and infinitives.
I employ words I remember
from German and Spanish,
I speak English when the story
becomes complex and difficult
though the words themselves
are plain and simple.
My five angels understand best
when I make wild and mysterious gestures
with my hands, when I beat my fist
against the coffin of my heart
or fall silent,
and they have only to look in my face
to see how far I've come,
to see my heart is broken.

2.

As the sun goes down,
I tell them a story,
make them swear never to repeat it,
telling the story only in English
to emphasize feeling over fact.

"I saw something very strange
today in Rome," I tell them.
"I was passing the time between trains
in the gardens of the Villa Borghese,
sitting on a bench, eating ice cream.
A man walked toward me down the gravel path
near the stalls of the *carabinieri*.
Smartly dressed, handsome, he seemed
carefree, tossing keys in his left hand
and humming under the linden trees.
A moment later a woman rushed through the gate,
running toward him,
awkwardly carrying her coat
as her shoulder bag bounced and knocked against her.
She was screaming; he ignored her
and kept walking.
I thought perhaps that he had said something to her
on the street before entering the garden
or had been forward on a crowded bus,
that she came now for revenge,
to defend her honor,
that he would feign innocence,
swear he'd never touched her.
When the woman caught the man,
she dropped her coat and bag,
spun him around
and beat him with her fists,
scratching his face,
clawing his eyes.
And the man did nothing
except close his eyes
and hold on to his broken glasses,

absorbing the blows like a saint,
like a martyr.
It was then I realized
he loved her,
she was his wife,
that she too must have loved him very much
to attack him this way in a public park.
She beat him until there was no good in it,
until he turned away
and, his back to her, began to weep.
She stepped back, yelling,
hurling questions at the wall of his back.
He turned. Unable to meet her eyes,
he said something so softly
only she could hear.
Then she took a step forward,
wanting to hit him again,
raised her fists,
but fury had left her
and the man walked away
down the path in sorrow.
She followed,
but not before she bent to pick up
the keys he had dropped in the dirt,
the keys he would have forgotten
and lost
had she not been there."

I ask the Italians if they understand.
No one says a word. Now,
I tell them, I will finish the story,
this parable, this little novel,

reminding them of their vow
never to repeat it.

"The man and woman walked to the stables
where they studied the horses of the *carabinieri*.
The proud horses — usually aloof and haughty —
returned the lovers' gaze with patient brown eyes,
tossing their heads sympathetically
like priests.
                    And though I had no right
to follow the lovers with my ice cream and notebook,
though the lovers' novel was written in Italian,
I eavesdropped as the horses spoke,
as horses in Italian novels sometimes do,
forgiving the man his infidelity,
the woman her inability to forgive.
The horse-priests said,
La passione è difficile,
and offered themselves
as models of discipline.
The horses said their lives were a novel
full of grain and wind and sweat.
They told of men in blue uniforms
who arrive with the light each dawn
to wash and brush them,
bringing fresh straw.
The horses said they love each day,
galloping through the woods
or walking slowly by the villa's open windows
so their riders can admire the lovely sculptures,
the horrible *Rape of Persephone,*
the terrible *Apollo and Daphne.*

The horses said they don't understand
the human love
of stories in marble and bronze.
They understand only
that each day as they enter the woods
with light falling through trees,
with leaves under their hooves,
their hearts become so full they think
if they don't die right then
they will surely live forever.
And when the horses fell silent
and bent their heads to the sweet water
flowing fresh down the long wooden trough,
the lovers turned away,
perhaps toward home,
where they would make love,
touching each other gently and with respect,
then with increasing passion and need,
healing each other simply
with their love."

In the compartment,
the baker, nun, fisherman,
and tiny old couple
listen to each word,
leaning forward when I whisper,
nodding at a word they understand —
carabinieri, Bernini.
But I am finished talking;
I will say nothing more in English.
But they don't know that yet,
and watch me and wait to see if the story continues.

When I finally lower my head,
open my book,
and continue reading,
they don't wait for my tears;
they argue over the meaning of my story,
yelling at one another,
waving hands, interpreting,
translating, revising, editing, embellishing,
digressing
into the mystery
of lives they have observed,
adding their own emotions
and personal histories
as if they've comprehended everything I've said
and no longer need to consult me,
talking among themselves now
as if I had disappeared.

3.

Just before midnight,
we take turns in the WC
with our toothbrushes and our washcloths.
When the coach lights go out,
the nun vows to watch over me
as I finish my book by flashlight,
but she's a tired angel
and falls asleep in a minute.
The old couple curl
on their seat like two cats—
they're that small.
The baker snorts and snores,
hands on his belly,

A Perfect Time
181

face white as flour in the moonlight.
But Rafael, the fisherman,
is too young to sleep.
He stands outside in the corridor,
admiring the moon and moonlit water,
thinking,

I will tell my friends
what I heard and saw on my journey.
I will sit in my uncle's café
and my cousin will bring wine and glasses.
We'll drink to the moon
bathing the rocky coast of our village
and to spells the moon casts on fish
we catch in our nets at dawn.
I will tell my friends about the strange American
and how fine it is to stay up all night
admiring the moon,
admiring the moonlit water.
And I will tell them how,
when the entire train was dreaming
except for the American
hidden behind his book and flashlight,
I saw an old man in the next compartment
sitting across from his daughter,
admiring her as she slept,
tenderly, secretly watching her,
biting his knuckle now and then,
so astonished was he by her beauty.

Cathedral

Songbirds live
in the old cathedral,
caged birds bought at the street market
and freed as a kind of offering.
Now doves and finches and parakeets
nest in the crooks of the nave's highest arches,
roosting on the impossibly high
sills of stained-glass windows,
looking down into the valley of the altar
as if from cliffs.

Twice a day, you'll hear them singing:
at dawn
when the blue light
of angels' wings
and the yellow light of halos
flood into their nests to wake them;
and during mass
when the organ fills
the valley below with thunder.
These birds love thunder,
never having seen a drop of rain.
They love it when the people below stand up
and sing. They fly
in mad little loops
from window to window,
from the tops of arches
down toward the candles and tombs,
making the sign of the cross.

If you look up during mass
to the world's light falling
through the arms of saints,
you can see birds flying
through blue columns of incense
as if it were simple wood smoke
rising from a cabin's chimney
in a remote and hushed forest.

The White Star of Hope

At the height of the storm's fury,
I lay in bed,
feverish, delirious,
willing at last to surrender
all my illusions
of happiness
and pass from the world unnoticed....

Outside the window—
towering thunderheads,
anvil clouds,
and a white flower with five pointed petals
blooming on the hill beyond my window,
silhouetted—
when the lightning flashed—
between sea and sky.
Delicate as a lily,
it was the only flower
left alive on the barren island,
the only flower to survive
African storms
and winds sweeping down from the Alps.

If I was going to die,
this flower—
this little White Star of Hope—
would be my last religion,
more beautiful than the earthly rose,

more graceful than the spiritual poppy.
I put all my faith
in five white petals tossing in the wind,
closed my eyes,
and slept.

On the third day, my fever broke.
I drank some onion soup,
felt my strength returning.
According to the laws of my new religion,
I opened my door and weakly climbed the hill
to offer a stone of thanks
but the White Star of Hope was gone.

Had my flower walked
across the water, across the mountains
to the door of another deathbed?
Had I truly seen the flower?
Or was it only a dying man's dream,
a simple vision that visits souls
after terror passes
in the final hours of peace?

Then I saw the clouds, too,
had vanished.
The storms had passed;
the sea was calm.
The sea and sky will change
and remain the same
forever,
as I shall,
wandering in the mountains,

steadfast in my faith.
Along roads scarring the valley
or shepherd paths climbing the hills,
I kneel by the wayside
and construct an altar
for other weary travelers
in need of a place to worship,
as I was in need, sick and dying,
propped up on my pillow, studying
the White Star of Hope through the window.

Saved by a flower,
I now build altars of stone,
small mounds of rock
bearing a twig
or a bramble
studded with five torn pieces of paper
on which holy words are written—
hope, faith, love, everlasting
glory—
torn pages
tossing in the wind,
a white star of hope
covered with salt and dust.

Mortification of the Flesh

The words come from nowhere
like stars so bright, so perfectly constellated
they seem an unmistakable command
clearly translated from the unknowable
language of God:
dive off the cliff in the dark.
After a month at my desk,
lost in the world of the spirit,
lost in the world of the mind,
I unbutton my shirt, feel
a shiver of cold air on my chest.
For the first time in days I listen
to the storm raging outside.
I open my door and rain rushes in,
scattering across the floor like blowing sand.
I leave my desk with its bright light and books
and start out blindly down the hill across the meadow,
abandoning my shoes,
stumbling as I take off my pants,
rain lashing my body, wind punishing me,
brambles and briars tearing my skin.
I climb rocks like a goat
to a ledge at the end of the world,
the face of the cliff
ravished white by lightning—
the voice says *dive!*
Below me, the sea
throws itself on the rocks,
unable to bear living forever.

Dive off the cliff!
Mortified, my terror trapped
between rocks and waves and rain,
I take off my glasses,
ultimate gesture of the lonely intellectual,
and scream like a madman, a lunatic angel,
"I am the King of Sicily!
I am the Eight of Wands!
I summon the devil! I summon death!
I command the night to behold my body,
this glowing angel, this luminous chariot!"
My name married to thunder and wave,
I open my arms to the storm,
and leap,
my glasses in my hand.
I dive from the cliff like a hawk,
fly through the air like a falcon,
drop in the sea like a gull.
Salt of darkness, blanket of thunder,
distant explosions of waves.
Fierce currents rock me like a mother
but it's too late:
I'm dead.
I'm seaweed, salt,
an empty shell rolling over the desert of the ocean floor.
Like any drowned thing, my body
washes onto the shore of the world.
My hands bleeding,
my feet bleeding,
I crawl over knives of coral,
I lie on blades of rocks,
half human, half fish,

singing softly,
praising the mortal body,
honoring astonished flesh,
blessing rocks,
blessing furious waves,
giving thanks for wind and rain,
leaving them to struggle without me.
In the meadow, over the graves of my shoes,
I stand and bless the storm, bless bloodied hands,
cliff and lightning
and the sea from which my life is resurrected,
my spirit redeemed.
Climbing the hill,
my face in the rain, my feet in the thorns,
I put on my glasses and see
the stutter of a yellow light—
my door
banging open and shut in the wind,
the light from my desk
a beacon guiding me
back up the hill,
back to my house,
back to my pens and books.

The Cave

After climbing the hill,
after leaving a trail
ragged as a scar
through thick yellow grass
and wildflowers wet with dew,
after basking all morning
like a lizard on a hot stone
high above the dazzling sea,
after squinting for hours
into bright, flawless, empty sky
until the sun had burned
every dream
from my sleepy eyes,
I foolishly thought
it would be easy
to turn from light
and enter the cave.
I thought
it would be nothing
to abandon my shadow
and marry darkness,
to descend into gloom
and suffer
the underworld's cold
murky tunnels
and narrow passageways.

The mouth of the cave
—sunstruck—

seemed the portal
to a secret temple
carved into the mountain
centuries ago, a temple
flooded with eternal light;
but the twisting tunnels I wandered
soon became a labyrinth,
the way uncertain,
as darkness
swept over my body
like black water,
like night sweeping through the cavernous
space between stars.
Lost,
my sightless hand
held out to whatever was there,
my foot inched forward in dust....

Finally,
I stopped,
placed my hand
on my pounding heart,
and listened
to the rush of each breath—
its echo
a quiet litany
whispered back by the void.
Then I understood
why I left
the green and yellow world,
why I abandoned
the day to live

in a temple
of darkness:
perfectly still,
quietly breathing,
hand on my chest,
I closed my eyes
and inhabited
the lightness of each moment,
the perfect union
of heartbeat and breath,
the miracle of the body
which is
and forever shall be
the poem
against loneliness and death,
world without end....

Eyes quieted
by darkness,
I turned
and began the slow
ascent,
trusting the path
of dust, trusting
the trembling world
to be there
—shimmering—
noon's bright promise
fulfilled
as the tunnel opened
into wide chambers
and dusky light,

walls adorned
with hieroglyphics
of carved hearts
and chiseled names,
hard floor littered
with broken bottles,
bits of clothing,
charred circles,
flashes of sunlight
and my shadow,
the black cross of my body,
breathing in, breathing out —
heart radiant at the mouth of the cave.

Pirandello's Shirt

In spite of the black mask
and thin black mustache
painted on with Magic Marker,
I recognized Pirandello
when he climbed through my window,
meowing and curling up at my feet to nap.
Just one or two hunks of cheese,
a slice or two of prosciutto,
and he follows me everywhere
like a starving dog, racing past me
every night on the stairs
like an alley cat
anxious to watch the moon rise.
On the roof I dip some bread in wine—
I'm willing to share—
but his hunger is terrifying,
especially considering the fact
he's been dead fifty years.
We strike a bargain,
nothing to do with charity,
nothing to do with gifts:
I keep my bed,
he sleeps perched like an owl on the garden wall.
On Sunday mornings, he leads me
to the edge of the cliff.
We wait for the lone truck to roar
from the village down to the sea,
where the fishmonger opens his door

and throws dozens of fish back into the water.
Some are frozen in solid blocks
and sink to the bottom
like stones from a temple,
a carved frieze of fish.
Others break free and float on the surface,
glinting like knives.
I tell Pirandello I've never read his plays,
I want to know what he wants,
why he's come back.
If he has some message,
I demand to hear.
I threaten him, make a fist,
grab his shabby suit and shake him
until there's only a black shirt in my hand,
which I put on to fight the chill,
a shirt the color of night,
the shirt that will make me invisible
as I sit here for a thousand years
watching the rituals of hunger,
rituals of life and death,
birds flying, their savage symphony,
the dead caught in their beaks,
the dead hanging from their talons.

The Hermit

I'm sleeping on my red-tiled roof,
a roof garden rich with bougainvillea
cascading like a waterfall over the ledge.
I'm sleeping between pots of pink geraniums
and boxes of blue forget-me-nots,
one ear to the silent world of my house,
one ear to heaven's white rush of stars.
Curled on my side like a dog,
I'm finally content —
my closed eyes two smiles,
fists under my chin two wildflowers
ready to blossom. Here beneath the stars,
I'm dreaming of the past, remembering
the house I slept in when I was young
and saying my first good-byes.
I see my mother in bed dying,
my father the pilot leaving again
to fly through the country of air.
I see myself washing happiness from my hands
in the cold stream that swept down our hill.
I'm drinking the clear water;
I'm slipping and getting my shoes wet.
I'm wading upstream into the forest,
seeking the place where a recluse dwells
by the din of a hidden waterfall.
From the doorway of his shack,
the old man — bearded, gaunt,
wild from long years of solitude —
watches me climb the rocky path,

his fierce eyes fixed on me
as I approach
and ask his name…
ask again….
But the hermit can't hear,
having lived long
by the deafening water.
All he hears
is an endless rush,
a sound like wind
or God.
He puts his finger to his lips
and says,

Shhh…
    listen—

Dancing

I'm dancing to drums of distant thunder,
my bare feet raising clouds of dust
on the dirt street in front of my house.
I'm dancing with the island's two bony dogs
and the harbor's thirteen starving cats.
I'm singing a song of thanks to the bat
eating the singing mosquitoes,
watching them all blindly diving
through the streetlamp's yellow sea of light.
I'm crooning to the clouds
rushing in from the East,
asking if they speak English,
asking will they marry me.
Above the mountain, lightning flashes;
the sea turns itself to stone.
The sea thinks rain is an insult.
But I love the rain.
I love the rain on my face like a thousand kisses
when I'm dancing and the sky is black.
I love it even after I've been abandoned,
after the dogs are gone, the cats,
after the bat has flown back to its cave,
back to the heart of the mountain.
The door to my house is open,
my books spread out on the table.
The wind blows—
pages flutter, crazy with knowledge.
My notebook shuffles its pages,
looking for a poem about winter,

looking for a poem about death.
The house says, "Come in, it's cold,"
but I don't know if the house means
the storm
or its own yellow light.
So tonight, as the rain dies,
I keep dancing,
touching the world with my feet
here in the road
between my house and the raging sea.
My feet love stomping in the dust.
They love splashing in water.
Surely somewhere on earth
there must be a fire
where people are dancing,
dancing on coals,
preparing for the fire beyond.
Dirt road, muddy stream, circles danced around a fire—
all the same.
There's only one path to paradise:
my left foot—a cloud of dust;
my right foot—a mud puddle splashing!

The Siesta

Everyone knows it's no use to wonder,
but after three cappuccinos
I can't help asking
as I lie down
beneath my arbor of fig trees and grapevines,
what would have happened
if I hadn't slept all summer?
And how will things change
if Antonella says yes?
Blue washes over the courtyard,
saying it doesn't matter.
Now and then, according to the whim
of the breeze, sunlight through
holes in my green heaven dazzles me.
I don't know which I love more,
the grape leaves like giant clover
or the two suits of the schizophrenic fig,
half its leaves shaped like clubs,
half like hearts or spades.
The doctor says rest.
Antonella says love.
But who can sleep
or pucker up for a kiss
when it's impossible to tell
if the vines' dark twisting alleys
and the branches' broad highways
are paths that lead to the empire's decline
or roads that lead to glory!

The Temple

I'm building the temple
stone by stone,
raising statues of women,
raising statues of men.
I've constructed an altar
of oyster shells and olive branches.
Any peasant can make an offering—
rusty nails, bent and broken,
old keys that open nothing and go nowhere,
dead flowers, spent candles, poems.
My temple has no walls, no doors.
Sunlight flows between the columns.
All are welcome
to slip in and admire the moon,
or leave, if it's late and they must,
stealing across the meadow,
the hillside white with dew,
the city burning below,
knowing there is a god,
never looking back.

The Edge

It doesn't have to be terrifying.
Sometimes it's simply curling your toes
over the end of the high dive,
bending your knees and lightly bouncing
up and down, as if your wings were fluttering.

Or it might be the moment when you're waiting—
dawn—at the border—
for the man in the blue uniform
to hand back your passport,
to say it's all right to leap
from the train to the platform.

And after the flying and the splash,
after you haul your bag up on your shoulder,
it's safe to say that before long
you'll come to the edge of *something*
and have to leap again.

Maybe it's someone you didn't see
by the pool, wearing a flowered bathing suit—
maybe the love of your life.
Or maybe it's a museum with one painting
that finally explains everything.

And even if death *is* waiting,
you can still love
the perfect fit of the doorknob

in your hand as you open the door.
You can still search for the immortal
painting and buy postcards of it
to send all over the world.
You can leap
and let the water hold you,
throwing one hand over the other,
hoisting yourself up
to dry your body in the sun.
You can lift your rucksack—
the road rolling away before you—
and walk on joyfully,
going forward, forever leaping,
loving the high dive as well as the bottom stair,
loving the held breath, loving the tired feet.

On Suffering

Four in the morning in a quiet house
is like a clearing in a forest,
tranquil, serene, a perfect time
to ask forgiveness
or consider the future's empty face
rising like a new moon,
a good time
to rise from bed,
descend the stairs,
turn on the kitchen light
and warm some milk.
It's relaxing
to watch a pot of milk
slowly come to a boil.

At this hour,
it's easy to mourn
the infinitesimal world
of one's life,
the sad history of the heart.
Sitting on the side of my bed
sipping milk,
I turn out the light,
slip out of my slippers,
lie down,
and consider the simplicity
of the beginning,
the first word,
light.

I once read
that milk,
warmed,
is a sedative.
Do you believe that?
Do you believe falling asleep
is a form of death?
Waking,
a resurrection?
Do you know what I think,
drifting off toward dawn?
If, in the garden of the world,
there's such a thing as suffering,
I have never suffered.

48 Questions

How old were you when you wrote your first poem?

According to my mother,
I composed poems at age three, or four—
she can't remember exactly. She recalls
a boy lying on the floor of his room,
penciling stanzas in capital letters
between the ample lines of a notebook
long since vanished. My mother
cannot say now what I once wrote.
I like to think I composed odes
on the paradise of childhood,
and that lines endure, radiant still
in the blackness below memory,
the light from those poems
shining across a lifetime to touch me.

What is your favorite color?

Before the long winter comes,
I find it restful
to meditate on the end-
lessly subtle hues of green,

from pale heart-shaped leaves
of snow-on-the-mountain
to emerald-black
boughs of spruce in shadow.

I have seen no green on earth
not divine —
myriad crowns of trees
rich with leaves soon to die —

the summer serene
as the green of Laura's eyes.

What is your house like?

A spruce tree shades
stairs to the front door
trimmed with English ivy.
The baby's room is blue
like his eyes; our room
is white—simple and spare.
A gilt chandelier rules
the red kitchen, whose windows
open on an English garden
and the green table where we sit to eat.
In the bright basement, my library
and, taped to the walls,
unfinished poems—
beams of a book I am building.

Where did you get the leather bag you carry to your poetry readings?

Once upon a time I lived
without anything to carry my poems.
Then one morning a cow poked its head
through my open window, offering its services.
"I am a cow," she mooed, "and my life is free
from care. I like standing under a tree,
swishing my tail, munching sweet grass.
But for you
I will become a leather bag
so you can carry your poems safe and dry."
"No, no, please don't," I cried,
but already I could feel
the leather strap across my back,
the weight of the poems she would carry.

How did you meet your wife?

Swimming the English Channel,
struggling to make it to Calais,
I swam into Laura halfway across.
My body oiled for warmth,
black rubber cap on my head,
eyes hidden behind goggles,
I was exhausted, ready to drown,
when I saw her coming toward me,
bobbing up and down between waves,
effortlessly doing a breaststroke,
headed for Dover. Treading water,
I asked in French if she spoke English,
and she said, "Yes, I'm an American."
I said, "Hey, me too," then asked her out for coffee.

In planning a manuscript how do you lay out the arc?

I lie in tall grass
in a meadow wet after rain,
my clothes soaking, the sky
like a blue hole inside me,
and calculate the time
clouds take to unveil mountains
after the storm has passed.
In this manner I measure
the arc of my soul,
while inside my house,
upstairs by an open window,
pages blow from the desk
and scatter across the floor—
a path of white stones.

Do you let go of a poem after it is published?

Once
I lost myself
in one of my books
written long ago.

The poems seemed the poems
of a stranger:

> *the child is calling*
> *the pain which will come*
> *and by which his life*
> *will be defined....*

I stood alone
in the quiet room,
the book in my hand,
astonished at so much suffering.

Where, when, and how do you write?

A line alights—
I wake,
catch and keep it in the dark.
Days I scribble in a notebook
carried in a leather bag.
At my desk I type draft after draft,
search for each line's ideal form,
tape endless revisions to the wall.

Or I lie motionless on an iron bed,
half-asleep, half composing,
a lamp burning in my head,
poems and dreams
swirling in the mind's alembic
while sun and moon move in their orbits.

What do you do when you say
"to hell with it" and leave your work?

When a poem I'm writing
stalls and goes nowhere,
I use that as an excuse
to turn off the desk lamp
and slip out the back door
to stand among long shadows
in moonlight, a shadow leaning
against the woodpile, slowly
breathing drafts of cold air,
gazing into the sky where
numberless stars have died
and where in endless night
new stars—like poems—
from emptiness are conceived.

Could you talk about the tension between the concrete and the spiritual?

Every day I boil water for tea,
sit down at the table to drink.
I try not to think of anything else —
poems, Laura,
those who died, those who live —
only my cup of tea.

But sip by sip
I lose myself
in the lines of a poem
I'm still revising —
all summer I lay in fields of clover —
and I hardly taste the tea,
even though the tea is sweet,
even though the tea's delicious.

Comment on this: in the real scheme of things, poetry is marginal.

All things —
the empty wine bottle under the bed,
the silver brush on the vanity,
an untended garden behind an empty house,
willow branches, a handful
of dirt thrown down in the grave —
all things flow one into another
like lines of poems that take me
to the far reaches
of myself
where I meet you.
Remember:
when Emily Dickinson said,
"I'm nobody," she spoke for us all.

T.S. Eliot said something to this effect:
"Steal from the best." What have you stolen?

I
have
stolen
my
mother's
mourn-
ful-
ness
and
my
father's
lone-
li-
ness.

Besides books, what do you collect?

Foreign coins,
skeleton keys,
old French primers,
small tin boxes —

any little thing
I can hold in my hand
that like a prayer says
be attentive

this is the way we live —

bits of blue glass
polished by waves
and saved
in a jar
in a drawer.

Who is your muse?

I'm shy around women,
but of the nine muses, I like best
old Martha Dunbridge, my sweet neighbor,
who brings chicken soup when I fall ill.
And reclusive Aunt Mabel, whose lush garden
attracts rare butterflies. And Mary Alice,
my first love, who cared nothing
about her beauty but always bared her soul.
The others I don't think I've met,
though at a cocktail party
an agent once introduced me to
Roberta Simon, muse of distressed souls,
who long ago traveled to Sweden,
back when her name was still Robert.

What effect has your new son had on your writing life?

While Andrew sleeps
in the room that used to be my study
I go downstairs to a desk
in a corner of the basement
to write. And each day when he wakes
I sit him in my lap and keep working,
bouncing him on my knee and typing
like I used to, quickly with one finger,
reciting lines to see
if my poems put him to sleep.
That's heaven — writing poetry,
Andrew in my arms. Though I abandon
the most divinely inspired poem when
Andrew wants his bottle.

Who will people read in 100 years?

Renée Le Calme (born 2053),
the Parisian prodigy who shall marry in poems
the sacred and the profane,
embracing the temporal world while singing *la poésie pure*:

> *dans cet hiver sans fin une femme dort,*
> *sa bouche une rose, meurtrie, rouge,*
> *rêvant son amour pour le Dieu dans l'extase*

> *in endless winter a woman sleeps —*
> *her mouth a rose, swollen, red —*
> *dreams ravished by the longing of God*

— TRANSLATED FROM THE FRENCH
BY BARTON VON MUNSTER
FROM RENÉE LE CALME'S POSTHUMOUS COLLECTION,
Hiver sans fin, (EDITIONS GALLIMARD: PARIS: 2103)

How do you situate yourself regarding narrative and lyric poetry?

"I'm glad you asked that," replied the narrative poet, leaning on the lectern, wondering if he hadn't been asked that question before, and what he had answered, trying to remember the woman's questioning face, her name, the dress she wore. She'd asked the question one day after church—she, too, she'd said, was a writer. His mind spinning the question, he began to compose the opening of a thousand-page epic: *The rumpled poet stood on the podium, blinking red-rimmed eyes under the harsh stage lights, ignoring his audience and remembering....*

Meanwhile, unnoticed, lyric poets listening in the dark rose from their seats and quietly ascended in slow procession the carpeted aisles of the crowded auditorium, opening doors and slipping away to dream beneath the sky, listening for names of new constellations shimmering in the eye of the night.

What do you do about dry periods in your writing?

When the writing is going well,
I am a prince in a desert palace,
fountains flowing in the garden.
I lean an elbow on a velvet pillow
and drink from a silver goblet,
poems like a banquet
spread before me on rugs
with rosettes the damask of blood.
        But exiled
from the palace, I wander—
crawling on burning sand,
thirsting on barren dunes,
believing a heartless mirage no less true
than palms and pools of the cool oasis.

Are there poems you won't publish?

Even C.P. Cavafy—
cynical, ascetic,
unknown in his day—
printed at his own expense
poems no one would publish,
poems intimate, personal,
to share with readers
he called friends.

But I have hundreds of poems
hidden away in a box.
Even when I know
Cavafy once wrapped verse
with black and gold ribbons
to give away as a gift.

Discuss your childhood experience with language.

1. MOTHER

To know
what I was saying,
she read my lips,
holding my face in her hands
like a book
so she could hear
what my heart was saying.

2. FATHER

I lay in fields of clover,
studying jet trails
as if
high above
in blue silence
he had written
love with nothing but air.

Have you written much prose?

Poetry is the horizon line,
the marriage of sea and sky.

~

On a desert island
a woman sleeps
surrounded by waves and sea
and countless clouds
crossing a brilliant sky
that vanishes in boundless space.

~

Climbing to the crow's nest
the horizon drops,
revealing the sky below
and unseen islands
with black lines rising—
smoke from signal fires.

What do you think of computers?

They say the brain
is a computer storing data
each moment in life.

If so, I could bring back
London, 1953,
and the hired nurse

who snatched me crying from the cradle
and shook me.
I could retrieve my mother,

rushing to the nursery
to fire the nurse on the spot.
Then I'd see my mother

consoling me, an image
I wish I could evoke now.

What is your favorite body part?

I love my baby boy's chubby thighs—
two plump drumsticks—
and the potato chips of his ears,
and the sweet spot
between his neck and shoulder
where he hides the sugar.
And I like my wife's voice,
its timbre when she talks to our son—
zephyr-soft and tender.
Some nights when writing
I let vanished voices go,
lift my head and listen
to this mother with her son,
this voice I've never known.

Talk about audience.

Before the advent of audio books
I volunteered to read to the blind,
going Sundays to the home
to read in the old-fashioned parlor
if it was cold and raining,
or when the day was warm and fair
to lead them outside to the lawn
to sit on benches and chairs.

I'd sit with my back to the sun,
wearing my dark glasses, looking up
from the glare of the page
to see them lift their chins
the better to listen,
or just to enjoy the sun on their faces.

What are you not telling us?

I'm not telling you about the brown dog
that followed me home from school each day—
an early death from my childhood.
And I'm not telling you whom I kissed,
the color of her hair, her favorite song,
what she said in her letter.
I'm not telling you about the dogwood
that bloomed on the hill by my house
and the blue vase with its tangle of branches,
the petals falling all night like snow,
shining on the floor in the moonlight.
And—because I don't know how—
what I felt that cool summer day
as my mother and father walked away.

What do you think of workshops?

My workshop has a wall of tools—
hammers, wrenches, handsaws, drills—
and shelves loaded down with screws
and nails, nuts and bolts, blades and bits.

I make frames for paintings,
endless miles of bookshelves,
and tables built from salvaged wood,
like my dining table, long and narrow,

spare and unadorned, with room for twelve.
Dinner with wine and friends
is much like a poetry workshop,
the ritual gathering of minds and hearts

around a table, the struggle to hear
what someone else is trying to say.

Do you perceive a difference between male and female writers?

A woman has a body
open to love,
a womb to nurture life,
and breasts which let down milk
like streams of vowels
into the hungry newborn's mouth.

Men's bodies aren't like that.
A man has a penis
like an extra finger to drum on the table
to stress the beat of an anapest or dactyl,
and pyrrhic testicles that go unnoticed—
two unstressed syllables.

But in the writer, man & woman—
as in the angel's glorified body—are reconciled.

What do you do for exercise?

Walking an endless path that goes nowhere,
I think of Wordsworth, who composed
great poems walking the banks of the Wye
or crossing Westminster Bridge,
and Thoreau, ascetic transcendentalist
who wrote while he wandered Walden Pond,
and Frost, who on chilly fall nights
walked Stone Farm's stubbled fields,
tapping out with a stick sonnets in the dark —
poets who knew the aim is not progress
but *rescue of the self from the round
of existence,* as I would be rescued,
middays in the gym, walking my treadmill,
staring out a tinted window at a shopping mall.

What do you do to get away?

I take my dog, sleeping bag, food
to last a week, and hike into the woods
where a tiny cabin waits by a lake.
There are dry logs (and dry matches,
should we arrive in rain or snow),
a plywood bunk, rough-hewn table
and bench, a pot and iron skillet.
I light the woodstove, boil water
from a stream for tea, eat supper
slowly from a can by lantern light,
pour a little whiskey on the fire
of my heart, and sleep, my open palm
holding the moon of my face
as the lake holds the shimmering sky.

What is your favorite drink?

A martini,
straight up, very cold,
and, not to bruise the gin,
stirred. In summer
I prefer a twist; in winter,
three Spanish olives. I like
drinking in the Oak Room,
at the piano bar of the Drake,
or home in the company of friends,
though crystal-clear martinis
make me long
for a cabin in the woods,
kneeling at a brook,
cupping my hands to drink.

What is your worst fear?

What
is
your
worst
fear?

A wise man
once said
nirvana
is one's
true voice,
but look
how hard
we struggle
for words.

What have you bought lately?

An eighteenth-century
cast-iron French fireback
adorned with a relief of Prometheus
and shaped like the black tombstone
I someday see above my grave.
Chained on the barren mountaintop,
beset by the eagle
that forever devours his liver,
the rebellious god drapes an arm
lovingly around the eagle's neck —
a gesture of togetherness and volition.
They stare in each other's eyes
and into their future, knowing
the punishment and torment to come.

Which of Superman's powers would you pick for your own?

When I was young, I longed
to leap tall buildings, or crash
through a wall, or bend steel bars,
or fly in a flash to Jupiter,

but now I want the prudence
of the Man of Steel
who knows
the power of kryptonite.

Because if *I* were Superman,
safe in a Fortress of Solitude,
I'd be my own greatest enemy:
I'd fly around the world

to be near and hold
what weakens the heart and makes me human.

You paint. What have you been working on recently?

When the moon is new,
I go out to paint the stars,
working first with a palette knife,
layering strokes of black and blue,
then stopping to study the sky
and mix the colors of starlight.

But dawn reveals canvases
neither night nor stars.
I've painted willow branches
dipping in tenebrous water
stirred by swimming swans,
or the mirror on my mother's vanity
shimmering in the dark with light
waning from a young boy's face.

What do you like musically?

The technical term is
calando, the gradual decrease
in tempo and volume at the end of a song;
or *niente,* "nothing,"
or *quasi niente,* "almost nothing,"
when the orchestra fades imperceptibly,
or plays as softly as possible —
a respite to the ear.

I also like unfinished symphonies —
imagining what could be.
Like damaged Roman manuscripts
ruined by ragged holes,
the archivist reduced to writing in brackets:

[teething moths were here]

Is poetry autobiographical?

A ghost returns one morning
to his old bed to rest,
but cannot rest, can only mourn
death failed to set him free.

Stripped of masks
and costumes
to keep his sad heart hidden,
the ghost walks again
through the town he died in,
remembering how he lived—

thinking, not being,
each heartache quickly denied,
pretending all night like an actor
who no longer has tears to cry.

Why do poets write?

My wife, a psychiatrist, sleeps
through my reading and writing in bed,
the half-whispered lines,
manuscripts piled between us,

but in the deep part of night
when her beeper sounds
she bolts awake to return the page
of a patient afraid he'll kill himself.

She sits in her robe in the kitchen,
listening to the anguished voice
on the phone. She becomes
the vessel that contains his fear,

someone he can trust to tell
things I would tell to a poem.

What has writing in common with dance?

—the solitary
dancer
alone in
her studio,
body poised
before
the mirror,
listening
for music
that joins
the earth
beneath her
powdered feet
to heaven—

What else would you like to be?

The bird—
a single black word
against a blank page of sky—
circling
in wide zeros
cliffs
high above water,
soaring, drifting,
wings opened wide
to its country of air,
flying all day
through empty sky
to alight
on a branch of the world.

Why do you read?

Whitman for spirit,
Issa for acceptance,
Dickinson for wit,
Milton for intelligence,
Larkin for cynicism,
Dante for pleasure,
Rilke for inspiration,
Wordsworth for meditation,
Frost for darkness,
Akhmatova for heart,
Hikmet for being,
Carruth for nothingness,
Rimbaud for ardor,
Shakespeare for humanity.

What major shifts have occurred in your work?

When young
my theme
was death.
Someday —
words burning
with electric life —
I'll praise
poetry,
love
& my wife's beauty.
But now I speak
for the heart
that needs
its God.

Has teaching affected your love of poetry?

Sometimes students skim poems,
spend time on things
they feel are more important.
Yet I know

poetry is like bread and breath,
and take solace in believing
the most jaded student
might remember

a poem he heard once in class,
opening his old textbook,
if he hasn't sold it,
to furtively copy in longhand

I hid my love to my despite
to send to the woman he loves.

What is the most foolish question you have ever been asked?

The Latin root
of "question"

means to seek or search,
hence *quest,*

a word we associate
in literature

with fools and dreamers,
their every question calling

to the universe for reply,
their every inquiry

magna quaestio —
that crying out

which defines our lives,
a cry rarely answered.

How do you begin a poem?

A horse charges across the plain—
a red horse,
no, four horses—
the four riders of the Apocalypse.
Or I hear *a silver cup brims*—
but "brims" with what,
I wonder, and then write
"thorns."

> *Four horses*
> *thunder across a sky*
> *charged with flames*
> *toward a sun black as ash*
> *in which a silver cup shines,*
> *brimming with thorns....*

What gives you hope?

Rain falls
on the cedar gate
and its red sign
playfully warning
CHIEN MÉCHANT.

My sweet old dog,
infirm, deaf,
warm and dry
in her house
beneath the linden tree,
wishes for nothing
as she watches the rain,
content with the world
as it is.

How would you like to be remembered?

Carve
an epitaph
on bluest air,

words to be
washed away,

like mists
that rise
on summer
mornings
and burn away
by noon,

like dusty
summer evenings
washed clean by summer rain.

What do you think of the future?

I remember
the war in Vietnam —
helicopters, children, smoke —
and homesick soldiers
calling the States "the world,"
where mothers and girlfriends
went strolling in shopping malls
vast as cities, built in a time
we hoped to inherit space,
preparing our children
to live in many-tiered starships
sailing galaxies in search of Eden —
      one blue world, one kingdom,
      a garden to call *home*.

If you could no longer write, how would you express yourself?

I'd be the surfer, locked in,
riding inside the green curl
so those on shore might better see
the beauty of a wave unfolding.
Or I would guide the novice climber
on the path of ascent
as if we were a single thought
slowly crossing
the mind of the mountain.
Or I'd be a builder of labyrinths
to show the path leading
to the center
is the same path
leading back to the world.

a note about the author

He spends the day
on the riverbank,
gazing at patterns
of light on water,
studying rowboats
slowly sliding
away until they
vanish,
letting the current
ferry his thoughts
across the empty
afternoon, while
he sits, idle,
on the bottom of his upturned boat.

Paintings

The Painting

lines adapted from Thomas Hardy's
"A Wish for Unconsciousness"

I think I would like to be a small
painting of a summer meadow
on the outskirts of London,
a picture hung on a wall
that lives as nothing else at all;
I would feel no doleful achings,
I should hear no mother's call,
have no evil dreams or wakings,
no anger, sorrow, or grisly care,
if I were a small painting
of a mild English meadow
under an empty sky forever fair.

Home

I went back to the farmhouse
where for years I lived in solitude.
A smiling couple answered,
invited me in.

They'd painted the rooms eggshell white —
the blue room where I sat up nights,
the yellow kitchen where words came
for a sorrow buried by the light of each day since.

Years have passed. And yet,
beneath the face I showed these strangers,
old yearnings and passions abide,
like the Ming reds and moss greens
hidden under the eggshell white.

Fishing

Then, it was easy to believe
the sad world to be gentle.
Rowing toward shore, walking
through the meadow's yellow grass,
carrying a string of sunfish
to the kitchen's screen door,
I'd think of friends
leaving their houses
and driving the darkening
roads at twilight
to dine on my catch
on a linen-covered
picnic table
under the maple tree
by the lake,
where, all evening,
our faces shining
like dreams in candlelight,
we'd laugh and talk
about things that made us happy.

The Plum Trees

The wealthy old woman
who owns the villa
by the little farmhouse
we used to rent each summer
hired some men from Avalon
to plant tall pines and poplars
along the lane — two lines of trees
that now hide her exquisite orchard.

This would have been the last spring,
had you been here, for us to see
the plum trees that startle the sky
with clouds of white blossoming,
the last summer to mourn the way
the old woman leaves plums to fall,
one after another, for no one.

The Doghouse

On the coldest nights
when the sky was clear,
I'd let Blackdog go first,
watching her
disappear
behind the canvas
that swallows dogs
then flaps back
over the entrance,
keeping out the wind.
Then I'd bow down,
crawl into the dim
chamber redolent of cedar.
It took a minute to fathom
the diamonds of her eyes
as I curled in the dust —
body to fur, man to dog —
and let myself be blessed
by the prayers of a panting dog.
Wind howling in the genuflecting trees,
the human in me as small as a dog,
the infinite unknowable night was
a compassionate and tender hand
stroking dog and contented master
who gave up the day and slept.

After Work

Coming up from the subway
into the cool Manhattan evening,
I feel rough hands on my heart—
women in the market yelling
over rows of tomatoes and peppers,
old men sitting on a stoop playing cards,
cabbies cursing each other with fists
while the music of church bells
sails over the street,
and the father, angry and tired
after working all day,
embracing his little girl,
kissing her,
mi vida, mi corazón,
brushing the hair out of her eyes
so she can see.

The Daughter

She felt she'd be punished
for not coming to visit before,
as if coming each year with flowers
kissed and laid on the ground
would have sustained her father's love,
marked it like a stone to be found
again, never to be lost;

but when she found no grave,
no stone hallowed by his name,
she walked among a thousand strangers,
a woman alone among the dead,
free of need
and offering neither love nor deed.

Wan Chu's Wife in Bed

Wan Chu, my adoring husband,
has returned from another trip
selling trinkets in the provinces.
He pulls off his lavender shirt
as I lay naked in our bed,
waiting for him. He tells me
I am the only woman he'll ever love.
He may wander from one side of China
to the other, but his heart
will always stay with me.
His face glows in the lamplight
with the sincerity of a boy
when I lower the satin sheet
to let him see my breasts.
Outside, it begins to rain
on the cherry trees
he planted with our son,
and when he enters me with a sigh,
the storm begins in earnest,
shaking our little house.
Afterward, I stroke his back
until he falls asleep.
I'd love to stay awake all night
listening to the rain,
but I should sleep, too.
Tomorrow Wan Chu will be
a hundred miles away

and I will be awake all night
in the arms of Wang Chen,
the tailor from Ming Pao,
the tiny village downriver.

The Cripple

Today she claimed she was going
to the library — my wife,
who doesn't care to read the paper.

It's not that I can't make love.
She stopped loving me
before this,

before I found myself
rolling around the house all day in a chair,
making the floorboards creak.

When I send her off,
I tell her, "I love you,"
then sit all day by the window,

smoking cigarettes and calculating
what I can do to her broken heart
that hasn't already been done.

Boots

the Argonne, 1915

Hard to believe I once slept
all day, rising in late afternoon
to saunter down the boulevard
and linger in cafés, all evening
holding forth on love and poetry.
Now I rarely utter a syllable.
Now I feel lucky to get through
the goddamned day, to wash my face
with snow, or take off my new boots
and light a smoke. Spring rain's
turned the butchered world to mud.
In this muck, no one's going anywhere.
My helmet over my eyes, I sleep
like the dead mired in this trench,
as beside me my best friend slept
all winter, snorting and snoring,
before a sniper's bullet shut him up
and made a gift of his boots.

The Piano

Leipzig, 1938

I was playing Bach,
the Concerto in C Minor,

when they kicked in the door
and ran mad through our house,

overturning bookshelves,
scrawling obscenities on our walls.

After they'd gone
I knelt

before the smashed piano
and wept.

My husband raised me by the arms
and shook me —

angry at my tears,
angry I should love

a wooden thing
on such a night.

Didn't I know, he cried,
people were going to die?

Going to die, he said.
The following autumn,

when leaves fell in our courtyard,
he was taken away.

Now music that once made me happy
accuses and rebukes.

I cried
and never found words to tell him why.

After the Divorce

She had said yes,
agreed to see him,
this younger man,
and now they were parked
in front of her house,
sitting in his car,
radio playing low.
He was telling her
his ambitions and wishes,
eagerly looking ahead,
filling the night with his dreams
as she sat quietly,
wondering what she was doing.

In the shadowed two-room flat
shared with her mother,
her twins were sleeping
behind dark windows.
Taped to the glass
were crescent moons
and ringed planets,
cut by a child's hand
from colored paper.

She'd wanted the young man
to think she was listening,
but that's what held her —
those dark windows.
It was all she could do

to hide her melancholy
as he ardently talked
and fiddled with the radio,
searching for songs
about love
or what might happen between them.

Devil's Quarry

a novel

　　Turning in bed, he saw the hands
of the clock tower scratching time.
How long could a fake name and a room
in a soul-sick hotel protect him?
It was midnight, it was two, it was five
in the morning and the hands of the clock
were lifting the pale sun from a grimy sea
to hang over the infernal city. His third day
without sleep, he rose like a ghost,
swaying slightly as he quickly shaved,
a little terrified to have to look at his eyes
for five minutes, ten minutes. The hands
of the clock tower called him, time was
running out. He had to leave the hotel room.
Open the door and descend the stairs. Had to
go out to the street where the day raged
like a deluge waiting to sweep him away....

The Empty Room

The dressing table held her perfumes,
powders and puffs, a silver brush.
A boy, I'd open the armoire,
find her white linen shirts folded
and smelling of lilac, simple cotton shirts
she wore hot summer days planting flowers.
On the top shelf, the white gloves,
a string of pearls, the blue silk blouse
she wore when she wanted to be beautiful.
I'd enter the room and touch the shirts
my mother lived and breathed in
before she died, before the cold
mirror emptied of her face
resumed crystal clarity.

Family

The day my cousin hanged himself
in his basement, his mother
called during dinner, and my mother
rose from the table to answer.

She stood at the window, looking out
at the night, listening to her sister,
while my sister and my father and I
put down our knives and forks, and waited

in silence, as was the family custom
when our phone rang during the evening meal
and one of us rose from the table to answer.

Early Life

I don't remember why
Mother dragged me from
the pew that April Sunday
and out the church doors
past a profusion of azaleas
extravagantly blooming,

and all the way home hit me
with the hard-handled hairbrush
she carried in her white purse.
I remember cringing under
the white-gloved hand raised high,
crying in vain for her to stop,

and being aware, as we struggled
down the street of our small town,
of crowds of daffodils turning away
as we passed the apple orchard
blossoming white as clouds in heaven
in the fields beyond our house.

Alienated

In front of the cottage, by the kitchen door,
deer come to nibble the bleeding heart.
Andrew and William tremble with joy
but I'm as distant as planes high above,
as vapor trails blowing away to nothing.

The Asylum

Somehow I knew it was there —
beyond the wall
down a pleasant tree-lined lane,
the locked windows calmly shining.

I pulled to the shoulder,
cut the engine,
and sat outside the closed gate,
thinking about living
in such a sympathetic place —
a pale-green room attended by doctors.

Cooling metal ticked.
Insects rasped in the trees.
Things unseen flitted in the night.

Snap out of it, I told myself,
starting the engine and turning on my blinker.

On the black highway,
blades of light cut the dark.
Snap out of it, I said,
I said
as I drove where I was going.

The Execution

Hands tied behind my back,
I must look like a man
with something important
to remember: what have I done?
I have loved my wife,
kissed my son each morning
while he was still asleep,
sunlight falling on his face.
The sun now on my face,
the bricks of the wall rough
against my back, my heart
beating so loud
I can't hear any more,
I see them laugh.
It's foolish to think
a blindfold could protect me
from eternity, hide the soldiers
from my eyes. I don't want it.
I want to see everything—
how it took me a lifetime
to learn to leave my dreaming,
to get out of bed
and put on my shoes.
Hands behind my back, last
cigarette between my teeth
pushed out at the soldiers
like a hot kiss, I remember

everything, the way
my wife laid me down on the grass,
the way my son jumped on top of me,
his laughter loud as guns.

The Voice

She remembers the evenings,
his eyes deep
in shadow,

his voice
desperate in the dark
as if life depended

on her,
her hand
touching his cheek;

but that was before
the world took him back
with its demands and obligations,

before he learned
to make love
in the hour before dinner

and to speak to her
in the same voice he used
to hail a cab, or call a waiter.

Triolet

When I asked what the spot on my X ray meant,
the doctor said, "You don't want to know."

But I knew what it meant.

When I asked what the spot on my X ray meant,
my wife was three months pregnant,
just beginning to show.

When I asked what the spot on my X ray meant,
the doctor said, "You don't want to know."

Reading with a Hangover

I close one eye but still can't
put the words together.
Each word is heavy,
not with meaning, but simply
the way it falls heavily
in my mind. Still, I keep
lifting words, turning pages,
dragging blood through my temples.
This is a book of poetry
I am reading. English poetry,
I think. I don't know
what the author is trying to
tell me. I can't understand,
can't think clearly this morning,
can't remember last night,
or how I ended up this way,
or what it was that made me so unhappy
it's worth feeling like this
not to know.

Young Woman, Paris, 1948

She remembered wearing red shoes
and a white dress, listening to
violins, and dancing with shadows
that fell on the winding paths
under the flowering linden trees
that ring the Jardin du Luxembourg —
a last waltz to say good-bye,
if only to the blue afternoon.

Later, alone in her room
above Boulevard St. Michel,
she took a bottleful of blue pills.
She lay on the bed looking up
at the high ceiling, waiting
beneath a fresco of sapphire sky
and clouds that seemed to glide.

The window lace breathed in
the last light. She closed her eyes
and rested a hand on her breast —
feeling the heart, waiting
for the soul to abandon the body —
and saw, as if from beyond,
a white dress hanging on its nail,
red shoes covered with daylight and dust.

Ninety-Year-Old Man

Philosophenweg, Heidelberg

A hired girl in white
pushes his wheelchair
through empty gardens
and up a steep cobbled path
that runs under an archway
of interlaced branches
to the quiet of the sky
and the esplanade's vista:
red rooftops crowded
below a towering steeple,
a blue-green river
crossed by ancient bridges.

On the Philosopher's Way
strolling lovers embrace
and disappear into the trees
while the old man and his nurse
linger by a low stone wall
gazing into the evening,
time flowing in waves
over the darkening hillsides.
I've lived so long, so much,
yet, foolish, I envy lovers
unhindered by memory and regret,
and pity my old heart too old
to be the lover of this young girl.

The sun disappears: the last light
suffuses clouds over the valley,
a heavenly fire paying homage
to the glory of mountains beyond.
When the dimming light finally fails
and unseen stars appear,
dispelling darkness,
the girl leans her face close
behind his shoulder
and pauses —
concerned about the deepening chill,
yet not wishing to disturb
what she imagines to be
his serenity.
Her breath warm on his cheek,
she asks if he needs anything,
his sweater, a blanket.

Indolence

Two in the afternoon, sprawled on the sofa
beneath the window, traffic too loud outside,
I sip whiskey with ice and read
a detective novel with the last chapter torn out.

Look at the floor, the floor, the floor,
littered with yesterday's headlines.
History is what we walk on, I guess,
when we get up for ice.

I could lie here for the next forty years,
staring at the ceiling, listening
to the ice maker in the freezer,
drinking my mother's milk.

But I'm like a deranged and demented dog.
Lying here reading my novel, I sip my drink
and something canine in me snarls, goes berserk.
I chase cars. I bite the tires.

The Punishment

In the empty street, the dog wanders
the parched gutter opposite the café,
then drops down in the dust to sleep.

She wonders aloud why the poor animal
doesn't find a piece of shade. The sun
is far too brutal, she says, too brutal.

He doesn't answer. He looks
for the waiter to order more drinks,
but the waiter's nowhere to be seen.

She says, When are you going to forgive me?
We'll talk about it later, he says. Unbidden,
the waiter reappears, bringing a jug of wine.

The café almost empty, the waiter
steps to the edge of the patio to smoke,
killing time, thinking *not enough tourists*.

In the gutter across the desolate street,
the waiter sees the same deaf mongrel
that's been scrounging outside the café all week

and, gleefully approaching the animal,
the same children who've tormented it
for days with their switches and sticks.

House by the Ocean

He slept on the sofa.
During the night it rained
and her dog, afraid of thunder,
lay on the floor beside him.
He rested a hand on the dog's back
and felt it trembling.

In the morning,
the sun came from behind clouds.
He woke, remembered
where he was, remembered
last night.

She sat drinking tea.
On the table she'd placed vodka,
a pitcher of juice.

She watched him rise from the sofa,
fumbling in the cushions
for his sunglasses,
squinting in the bright light.

She was the first to see —
beyond the resplendent glass,
just offshore beyond the deserted beach —
porpoises,
breaking the surface like thought,
like something someone wanted to say....

The Bedroom

The window was open
toward the water
and filled with light.

There was the sound
of boys on the dock,
sails luffing, rigging ringing
against the masthead.

The bodies on the bed
looked exactly
like the man and the woman
they had always been,

but already
that was the past,
which is over
and can never come again

though the window
was filled with light
and open toward the water.

The Game

Over tea, she asks what books
I'd choose, stranded on an island,

then whom I'd wish for,
if wishing could bring anyone,

naming her best friends,
my name not among them.

Then she asks whom I'd kill
if I could kill anyone....

I say
I can't imagine.

"I'd kill Brad," she says,
as if she were boasting, as if she had—

then pours another cup of tea
and complains that it's too cool.

The Test

That morning we
assumed names
and greeted the day
anonymous as stars
behind dark glasses.
At the clinic,
I asked for directions.
The receptionist
jerked a thumb
like a baseball umpire.
The room was small:
a teacher's wooden desk,
rickety old chairs
along a green wall.
For some reason,
I remember the nurse
wore a flowered dress.
She read our requisition slips
with the names we'd invented
and asked for payment
in advance, in cash.
She laid the money
in a small black box,
said, "Who's first?"
and locked the box
in the desk drawer.
She led me to a room
the size of a pantry.
There was a metal table

covered with needles,
small boxes, antiseptic.
From an old refrigerator
like the one in my aunt's kitchen
back in Carolina,
she retrieved a metal rack
constellated with test tubes
tagged with names and numbers.
"Make a fist."
She snapped the rubber tourniquet
tight. I looked at my arm
the way junkies do—
the vein rising.
I got nervous,
thinking of hospitals
where needles are precious
and the same one's used
on everybody.
The nurse laughed,
said something
reassuring,
and slipped the needle in.
Blood
pumped quickly
up the syringe.
"Hold this"—
a small round gauze
on the crook of my arm.
Then, for the first time,
I looked at the nurse's face.
"That's it. You're finished."
The nurse was writing

my fake name
on a stick-on label
as I left the room
to find my friend,
who waited on the edge
of her chair, searching
for something in her purse.
She looked like a little girl.
We were friends only,
never intimate.
But she would confide in me
and now she was worried.
She would be less afraid,
she'd told me,
to take the test with someone.
"Break a leg," I said.
The nurse held the door open.
When she came back
we hugged a moment
there in the room,
rocking each other
like two people
embracing in an airport
after years of separation.
Imagine: two people
lost to each other.
Imagine: believing
the one you loved
had disappeared
or had changed names
and you'd never find her again.
But we still had to wait

a few days more
for technicians to tell us
the end of our story,
what would happen to me
and to her,
whose name that day
was Laura.

To My Student's Father

A finger at her temple,
she pulls an imaginary trigger—
this is how your daughter answers
when I ask her how you died.
This is how she'll answer
the rest of her days,
the report of your gun
ending her life.
Her hand
drops to her side,
hangs there,
empty. She looks at me.
She's trying to see if I, too,
hear the gun go off.

The Scream

after Edvard Munch

The couple calmly walking on the bridge
can't hear the difference between your cry
and the river's terrible music,
a deafening song endlessly roaring.
The whole world is crying out:
sky and cloud, nails and planks
of the bridge you stand on.
Terror in the zeros of your eyes,
who will hear you
over the thunder of life?
Hands cover your ears,
but that won't help you. Let me
take your hands in mine, let me quiet you.
Listen: the world flows away under the bridge.

The Widower

After that day, he never again
visited his wife's grave.

FAMILY LEGEND

Seven years the farmer
honored his heart's appointment,
climbing each day
to haunt the hill that held his wife,

until one evening he saw
a mournful shade
rise from the ground that was her grave
and leave the earth forever;

then from his devotion
he turned away at last,
descended the hill,
and did not question

whether love was now the very air
or heaven the death of grief.

The Owl

after Guillaume Apollinaire

My poor heart is an owl
that is nailed, unnailed, renailed.
I'm through with blood and passion.
I praise all those who love me still.

Rain

There was a woman I once loved.
I lived with her one rainy summer.
I'd dream, or listen to music all day
in our room while she was at work.
She no longer loved me, I knew.
I'd walk to the park and study
the flowers in the conservatory.
I'd imagine a house where one day

I'd live, not so very differently from
the way I live now, working most days
on unrealizable poems, listening
to a composition by Rodrigo or Falla,
the guitar like a man in tears swaying
to music about love never dying.

Summer

After her bath, my mother
smelled like fresh linen,
like a field of lavender
or lilacs in spring.
Opening a small round box,
she'd powder her breasts
with a dainty pink puff
then pull her red robe tight.
If the window was open,
the lush crowns of trees
would rock against the sky
as if they, too,
knew she was dying.
She'd cross the bedroom
to her vanity and at the mirror
she'd slowly count to one hundred,
brushing her hair.
When I stood behind her
I thought I would break
if she touched my face
in the glass. I thought
if she leans closer to the mirror,
her breath will make me disappear.

The Distance

Sixty feet away,
kneeling in the grass,
my father made the strike zone
smaller, rocked back on his heels,
lifted the old, worn catcher's mitt
and held it steady,
waiting.

I held the glove and ball
against my heart. Winding up,
I'd look to first,
then whirl toward home
and unleash my fury.

After I'd thrown
one hundred fastballs
my father called *rockets,*
he'd hold the last pitch
and shake his head *enough.*

Then I'd walk
the distance toward him.

I never knew
what to say
when he'd rise
and I'd look at his frown
silhouetted against the azure

of coming night.
So I said
nothing

as he tugged the mitt
from his hand
as he did
so many summer evenings
and I saw
the damage I had done—
the blood-red palm
and swollen fingers,
the hand looking like
it would never heal,

though it was the hand
I wanted each night
to touch my face
and calm me.

The Weight

Blackdog, 1984–1998

All these years
I've never known
what Blackdog waits for
when we sit in the grass
and she looks sadly,
stoically into the distance.
But now the nights I lift her
shivering in my arms
carrying her into the house,
I know I carry
up the stairs
a trembling part
of myself.
I almost don't want to look
at her wizened body,
white whiskers, and cloudy eyes.
I almost don't want to nuzzle
her soft ears anymore.
It's too painful:
nothing I can do
will stop her tremoring.
I call her from the darkness
at the edge of the lawn;
she struggles to rise
and stiffly moves toward me.
I pick her up, care-
ful to support her wasted haunches,

strain as we ascend the stairs
toward the open door.
Sweet dog, good dog,
I say as we take each step,
remembering her
cradled in my hand, how light
she was as a pup,
before I learned
the weight of love
is also the weight of grief.

Paris

1. THE POEM

We ordered and the waiter left.
Then she showed me the poem,
written in French in ink on blue paper,
and asked me to help translate
into English—

> *J'attendrai,*
> *I will wait for you*
> *Beyond the waves of sorrow....*

2. THE ANSWER

Did the thief who stabbed
young Samuel Beckett
understand he was fated
to convey the answer?
When Beckett got out of the hospital
and visited the jail,
he asked the man why he'd done it.
"Je ne sais pas, monsieur,
je ne sais pas."

3. THE QUESTION

"Where are the souls
of the great French writers?

Paintings

Where is Victor Hugo?
Down what alley do the shadows
of Rimbaud and Verlaine disappear?
Beautiful language like a kiss,
upon whose lips do you now become
even more beautiful,
plus chaste?"
asked the old bouquinista
as she closed and locked
the heavy doors of her wooden bookstall.

Compassion

At dawn, a sparrow
on a high black branch, singing,
thinking spring has come.

୬

My old wooden fence —
gap-toothed, rotting, falling down,
yet younger than I.

୬

Kwan Yin stands alone
among the garden's flowers —
what is she thinking?

୬

I don't care how small
the ember is you give me —
it will start a fire.

Water

after Antonio Machado

Why call
those random paths
roads?
Everyone who walks
walks
like Jesus
on water.

Love

Driving home,
I couldn't help but fall in love
with the evening sky over the lake—
deep purple washed with blue
the color of my sons' eyes.
I was reminded of noon skies
infinite over the ocean
and desert nights thick with stars.
I saw Turner's vast skyscapes,
gray, silent skies before dawn.
I thought of the angry heavens
of *La tempesta,* a bolt
of lightning forever flashing
above Giorgione's soldier, mother, and child.
As I turned the car
into the alley behind my house,
Laura waiting in the window,
the motion detector blinded the twilight sky.
I remembered a Persian painting:
Krishna reclines in the Garden of Love,
his divine hands pleasing Radha's breasts.
Her hand caresses his neck
and draws him closer,
the radiant sky above the lovers
tranquil as the canopy of blue satin
above the bed where Vishnu dreams.

Blackdog's Ashes

In the top left pocket
inside my jacket
where I keep my pens,

under the bridge,
swirling
on wind and water,

and in the garden
where all these years
the roses have never refused
to bloom.

The Umbrella

It's raining and
the whole world
is dripping wet
with silvery rain
save the mother
and little boy
standing still
under a wide
black umbrella,
waiting for the
yellow bus,
perfectly happy.
The boy can't
decide whether
to look up
at the small faces
of rain tumbling
off the edge of
his mother's open
black umbrella,
or down at her blue
boots, the blue boots
with rings of soft
black fur that circle
the dainty ankles,
which, he sees,
even the raindrops
love, leaping
up from puddles
to touch her lightly there.

Flying

Like the terrible forgiving hand of God,
lightning
punched holes in the cargo bay
of my father's plane,
and like a devilish blessing,
St. Elmo's fire
danced on his wings.
Enemies shot at him,
and flak filled the heavens like black angels.
Once, with only one engine, he landed
a C-47 transport full of mules
on a runway lined with fire trucks.
My father flew through blizzards,
hurricanes, monsoons;
once, fierce hail stripped the green and brown
camouflage paint from the fuselage.
Camouflage, he says,
isn't much good
in a storm at 10,000 feet.
At Hickam Field,
in the spring following Pearl Harbor,
the base commander—
an aging, nearsighted colonel
wanting to fly again—
climbed into the pilot's seat
in the cockpit next to my father.
The sweetest touchdown of the colonel's career—
wheels meekly kissing the runway—
was a gift from my father

in the copilot's seat,
secretly landing the plane with his knees.
In a Stearman's biplane
in Ontario, California,
he learned to fly,
graduated to a BT-13 single-wing,
mastered a UC-78 twin-engine trainer,
and became a pilot in a B-25.
He logged more than a million miles.
Flew to the Azores, India, Greenland, Burma,
looked down on the Himalayas, the Alps, and Rockies.
Eighteen months he lived
in a thatched hut in the South Pacific,
and saw his buddies' plane plummet
in the sea off the coast of Fiji,
sharks in a feeding frenzy.
In China he woke to bombs
falling on the barracks.
He took R and R
in Paris, Honolulu, Cairo,
and has seen the Taj Mahal,
the Sphinx and the pyramids,
ridden camels
and flown under the Golden Gate Bridge.
After the war,
he was ordered
on a mission to the desert;
like a buzzard,
he circled
for days
in a plane as big as the ark,
ordered to collect

goats, horses, ducks
left in cages by the army
to test the after-
effects of the blast.
As a boy,
he pumped gas,
scooped ice cream,
and, with a friend who made coffins,
sealed crypts
in graveyards
in the Virginia lowlands.
Like Thoreau,
he once set the woods
behind his house on fire.
A career spent as gondolier
was brief—two days
rowing people through town
during the great flood of '32.
When he stopped flying,
he returned to his home
by the ocean. Retired,
he carved duck decoys,
painting them with an artist's precision—
his work admired and sought after—
but abandoned the hobby
after his grandson
drowned.
My father is eighty-three.
Now he has a garden
of tomatoes and mums.
Evenings before dinner
he drinks bourbon

ritually, in moderation,
tall glass, two fingers, ice, water.
He stays up nights reading
romance novels propped on his chest.
A Distinguished Flying Cross
hangs on the wall by his bed.
To this day,
no matter to whom he speaks,
he always says,
"Yes Sir,"
and remembers still
the name and hometown
of every soldier he met.
My father was a one-on-one pilot
with a green card.
He was never afraid
to give it the needle
and power the coal
and survived
one hundred and eighty-nine missions.
A million miles.
So very far.
When I come home
I ask to hear the stories.
I am his son—
a poet, husband, father, friend,
forty-six years old.
What I've learned about flying
I've learned from my father.

The Island

I speak English
but not with my mother and father's
soft, slow Southern accents.
In school I studied Spanish,
later dabbled in Swedish,
and still aspire to French,
whose music I love
but whose grace is beyond me.

When I lived on the island,
I kept to myself, a foreigner
in a stone house by the harbor.
Meandering through the market,
I learned the language quickly —
pane, pera, pesce....
At the kitchen table, I'd write
new words in a notebook,
memorizing useful phrases
while three kinds of pasta
cooked on the stove.

The island's limestone
had been quarried for centuries
and shipped to Rome —
Favignana was slowly
disappearing. I, too,
was an island
slowly disappearing

as the sun rose,
my life changed
by wind and water,
my past
fading like dew.
Night after night I'd lie
speechless on the roof garden,
listening to the keening stars
rushing through the night.

Along the Path

In line at the grocery:
a woman poised
with pudding

on her fingertip,
feeding her son,
who rode in the cart

like an Indian prince
surveying the morning
from atop his elephant.

Drove my guest
to her afternoon reading
which wasn't well attended

because, someone kindly said,
of the weather.
The reading, however, was lovely,

small and intimate,
like walking through a private garden
in the rain.

Before bed,
checking on William,
my head brushed against the mobile—

blue airplanes
soft as pillows
circling above the crib.

I could have lit the lamp,
but I didn't need the light
to show me what was there.

The Revelation

For weeks my labyrinthine walks
took me nowhere —
every day,
crossing countless small bridges,
every day,
disappearing down narrow passageways.

I had done nothing
to deserve it,
and yet it came nonetheless
in Venice,
of all places,
one night as I lay awake
by a threadlike canal
in the tiny Hotel Albergo.

It was like being born,
or being born again,
or dying into life.
I have no words for it.

I left the room
before dawn.
The wide lagoon —
in morning shadow —
lay empty and still.
Tied to mooring posts,
empty gondolas
black as coffins

waited in silken water
to convey the living
under the Bridge of Sighs.

When the day's first vaporetto came,
I paid and did not look back.
I did not muse on the story of Venice,
nor imagine the story that might come next.

The sun—
rising over a city of islands—
cast diamonds on the water,
and the windows of the palazzi were golden.
And I knew those shining windows could open
and anyone might look down and see
diamonds ablaze on the water,
that anyone who beheld me
could know my heart.

The Blessing

The Freight

Winter mornings I see
the ghost of my breath
when in my cold blue car
I turn the engine and slowly
back out of the garage,
looking over my shoulder
to see where I'm going.

My commute takes me south down Western
past car lots with white plastic banners
flapping like the wings of windblown gulls,
then down Peterson past the cemetery.
At Broadway there's always a traffic jam —
I sit awhile in the shadows of tall buildings.
But when I reach Lake Shore Drive, I race
along the ice-encrusted lake, rushing
through the middle years of life,
always anxious about being late.
Back and forth, every day:
my sweet rut.

This morning —
instead of turning in the direction of work —
on impulse
I went the opposite way,
driving north through falling snow
to the thrift store in Wilmette
to buy Andrew the bed
shaped like a race car —

a blue car with big, black wheels.
I'd seen it and wanted to be
there when the store doors opened.
I knew I'd have to pay,
carry the bed to the curb,
heave it to the roof and fasten it with ropes,
then drive home through deepening drifts,
wind buffeting my burdened car.
But I like thinking of him
sleeping in a race car,
the engine of his dreams and visions
carrying the freight of the soul,
and I've found that to make him happy
makes me forget my life.
Reconciled to being late —
snow falling heavier —
I drove home carefully,
going slow, his blue car
tied on top of my blue car,
one hand out the window, holding fast the ropes.

The Fear

I have a secret:
my little boy scares me.
He seems fragile
but barrels through the house
like a Sherman tank toppling lamps,
gleefully shrieking.
He loves the stove's blue flame,
tries to crawl inside the fridge,
dives headfirst into the tub.
He's learning to climb—
would fall out the window
if we didn't pull him back.

Last week, he got into some pills.
His mother and I rushed him to the hospital.
Prying a syringe into his mouth,
a doctor injected black chalk to save him.
That's what I see now:
my son in the emergency room
helpless on the table,
crying, screaming,
Laura holding him down,
the doctor shooting into his mouth
black stuff that looked like death.

He's okay; nothing more terrible happened.
All day in a quiet room divided by blue curtains
we tried to keep him still in the stark white bed.
From a tangle of wires adhering to his chest

a telemetry machine monitored his heart—
glowing lines of steady, rhythmic beats
like iambs running unstopped across the black screen,
a stubborn poem beating inside him
that cares not one bit about fear.

Father's Day

A few days after the storm
spared the beach house,
I spent the morning removing
the plywood that protected the windows,
balancing heavy, unwieldy sheets,
climbing up and down,
my eighty-year-old father steadying the ladder,
insisting he take a turn.

After lunch, when Andrew wanted to go
to the beach, my father stayed
in the cool, dark house,
content to spend the afternoon in solitude,
forsaking the sun for the silence of chores—
small tasks he could accomplish alone.

Carrying our son,
I followed my wife down
a long weathered boardwalk that cut
through white waves of radiant dunes.
On the beach, by sparkling water,
I bent down, one arm around my boy's waist,
and carefully rubbed lotion on his face
as he twisted and squirmed, trying
to break free, eager to build
a castle with his shovel and bucket.

All around there was nothing
but beautiful day, immense ocean,

Andrew with his mother digging in the sand.
I left them,
walked toward the water
and pushed through the shorebreak's rushing froth,
diving through churning waves
to surface—breathless—beyond the swells,
turning to site the tiny beach house
between the beleaguered world and open sea.

New Year's Eve

I go to bed early,
then rise
long after midnight
and drink milk in the dark
while snow floats down
beyond the window.

My fourteen-year-old
black Lab rouses,
staggers into the kitchen
to see what I'm up to
the first few hours
of the New Year.

Glad for her company
I offer the last
cold slice of pizza
but she won't eat.
She's shivering,
upset I woke her.

I go back to bed.
With great effort,
she slowly follows,
circling her blue pillow,
collapsing, curling,
sighing a deep good-night.

In sleep she unfolds
stiff arthritic legs,
shifting her paws,
claws clicking
lightly on the floor
as, in a dream,

she scoots
free of her leash—
running ahead,
though I call her name,
into woods of falling snow.

The Keats House

From the high window
of the blue room
in which you died,
I am watching
a group of girls
removing their shoes
to wash their feet
in Bernini's fountain
at the foot of the
Spanish Steps.
It is noon;
the fountain's pool
shimmers in the Roman sun,
the ancient light
falling on roof gardens
and ruins alike—
beautiful,
as the girls are
beautiful, laughing,
lifting their skirts
and happily resting
on the fountain's rim.
I wish you could see
their glistening ankles
as they dangle their feet
in the cool water.

The Poet's Mother

I met the poet's mother
in a coffee shop.
Frail, in her sixties,

she was sitting alone,
reading her son's book.
I asked if she was fond of poetry

(I'd seen the lines
broken on the page
as she rested the volume

to sip her tea)
and she showed me
the book's blue cover, his name.

I said, "You must be very proud."
She asked, "You *like* poetry?"
"Yes, very much."

She then put the book aside,
opened her leather bag,
and handed me two poems she had written—

one about a plane flying around the world,
the other about birds dying in cages.

The Roman

Fiercely striding the shady path
circling the park, he addresses
a companion I can't see. When
he stops in a shaft of sunlight,
a bruised white rose in his lapel
burns against his threadbare suit.
His gray hands petition the air,
gesturing toward lofty branches
of umbrella pines—those peaceful
green islands floating overhead.
Assuming his seat—
one of the park's wooden benches—
he majestically brandishes
a lush and fervid poetry, his voice
possessing an oracular clarity
possible only in Italian
and only in a Roman garden.
At the end of his speech,
under thick, sprawling branches,
the crazy man leans forward
and waits, silent,
affecting an attitude
not unlike mine as I study him—
scratching his beard, rubbing his chin—
as men do when they're listening.

The Seal

I keep my vow
not to break
the plastic seal
around the book
I bought in Rome
in the gift shop
of the Villa Borghese,
a study of Bernini's
marble sculptures
of mortals
grappling with gods,
an elegant volume
I carried for months
through Europe,
unopened
in my backpack,
the only thing
I brought home
from my journey,
something beautiful
I believed
could save me,
a book to open
like a locked door
inside my head.
Older now, I know
the absurdity
of my thinking:
a plastic seal

between life and death.
It's foolish,
but for safety
I keep the book —
seal unbroken —
on the nightstand,
always close at hand,
buried for years
under stacks of books
I've opened and know by heart.

Rest

What dwelling shall receive me?
THE PRELUDE

Past midnight, no place to sleep, I opened
the door to the shed behind Dove Cottage
and fashioned a bed of fresh, fragrant hay.
Head on my knapsack, shivering, I slept,
then woke, blinded by the glare of a torch,
two leashed Dobermans snarling at my face.

Under the ancient yews that ring the lake,
pensive and grave as young Wordsworth, I walked
the lonely lane he would have walked to town.
A wayside men's room was dark and bolted,
but the door to the ladies' room swung free
and I slept that night in the toilet stall,
a bright white guard-light in a metal cage
shining, for the moment, like a blessing.

The Blessing
342

Paradise Lost

Sometimes in dreams I see
the country of childhood —
the house and the garden
in which I played. I see
a boy lying in the grass,
a veil of rapture over his eyes.
I see the white lattice,
the indifferent roses
that climb like bloody hands
toward his mother's window.
Always in my dream
it is summer, afternoon,
and the boy's face is pale as frost.
His life is unraveling.
The world is
taking the shapes of words
he has yet to understand —
despair — loss — dread —

The Road

I, too, would ease my old car to a stop
on the side of some country road
and count the stars or admire a sunset
or sit quietly through an afternoon....

I'd open the door and go walking
like James Wright across a meadow,
where I might touch a pony's ear and
break into blossom; or, like Hayden

Carruth, sustained by the sight
of cows grazing in pastures at night,
I'd stand speechless in the great darkness;
I'd even search on some well-traveled road

like Phil Levine in this week's *New Yorker,*
the poet driving his car to an orchard
outside the city where, for five dollars,
he fills a basket with goddamned apples.

God

All year I have been praying, praying
and lighting votive candles—closing my eyes
to contemplate the white flames.

Look at me: I am in distress.
My heart is troubled, and in my house
there is none to comfort me.

And immediately You answer: "Yes,
tomorrow I shall make a new day,
a new year to be followed by the years to come,

but I haven't yet asked of you
those things you think
impossible."

The Blessing
345

The Storm

I called my father long-distance last night
to let him know how we're doing—
Andrew feeling better, the baby kicking,
me taking a turn with the flu, feeling like
I'm inside a glass bubble. My father patiently
waited for me to finish what I was saying,
then eagerly told me about the terrible
thunderstorm, asking if I could hear
the rain beating down. Suddenly
neither of us was talking.
I stood with the phone to my ear,
listening to drumming on the skylight
in my father's kitchen, picturing an old man
holding the receiver up to the thunder and darkness.

The Sermon

Instead of pouring the first glass of wine
I followed my doctor's advice
and took Andrew to the mall. All evening
we rode up and down the escalator.
In the food court we ate a baked potato.
Then we came home. I fixed his bottle,
and in the big striped chair in his room
we snuggled in the dark as he drank.
I whispered in his ear that I loved him,
and together we babbled
in his funny language under a heaven
of plastic stars glowing on the ceiling.
After he went to sleep, I made phone calls
I hadn't had time to make earlier in the day.
Then I walked through the house, turning
off lights. I turned off all the lights, save one
in whose glow I drank glass after glass of wine,
reflecting on a piece of a radio sermon I'd heard
on the way to the doctor's office, a sermon
about the Holy Spirit and what it means to be free.

And the Word

I find things inside books
borrowed from the library —
foreign postcards, rose petals,
opera tickets, laundry lists,
and, once, a bloody piece of cloth.

Today, inside a volume
of Cid Corman's elegant poetry,
a snapshot —
a man in a dark nightclub
embracing a red-haired stripper.

The man grabs the woman
brashly about her waist,
displaying her nakedness
to the camera. The flash
illumines the man's flushed face,
his single-minded lust
as he bends to touch
his tongue to her nipple,

while she, arching her back,
coolly turns to the camera,
her face flooded with light,
as if asking, "So,
what do you think
about the book you're reading
now?"

The Soldier

In a field hospital, tended by medics
and nurses who check red-stained bandages,
wounded and dying soldiers lie on canvas cots.
One soldier from the company sits

shaking violently, unable to raise his head,
his wounds not visible. The officers
rebuke him. But the wounded soldiers
know enough not to think him a coward.

The doctors' treatment: a handful of blue pills
to swallow. In two days—sedated, numb—
this soldier will be back at the front,
where suffering may end with a bullet.

"Elegy"

Walking in the woods, I saw
through a dark tracery of feathery branches
sunlight striking faded ribbons
hanging from pines.

The story made headlines last autumn.
The little girl had been found
here, her blackened body
bruised and burned.

In flourishing weeds lay
nubs of mourners' candles
and vases bearing stems,
the blossoms blown.

A moldering teddy bear
leaned against a crude cross
bearing hand-painted dates
bridged by life's short dash.

And, four small stones
marking the corners
of a decomposing poem
torn from a composition book,

only the title remaining—

Sunday Night

After they leave the restaurant,
the little girl's father
drives her home, says good-night

at the door to her mother's apartment.
Already it's late, past bedtime.
In her room, her nightgown

is laid out on the satin bedspread,
but tonight, once she's had her bath,
her mother lets her stay up awhile.

She plays with her dolls. Every night
she puts Mommy and Daddy in bed
together, watching over them and praying

to make sure nothing bad happens.
Then she tucks Baby into a crib
smaller than her very small hand.

Thirteen

After school,
we escaped
to a loft above
his family's garage,
where my friend
sniffed glue
from a paper bag.

He'd pass out
on a tattered mattress —
his eyes rolling,
his face ghostly.
I'd hold him
to the window
for air and see

his mother, busy
inside their house,
upstairs in his room
making the bed and
folding his clothes —
doing what mothers do
because young sons
still need them.

The Invalid

A young nurse spoon-feeds her
as her mother once did
though she has neither
appetite nor taste—
even for things

she once loved.
Plain vanilla ice cream
on hot afternoons.
A second glass of bourbon
on long winter nights.

What are seasons to her?
Bathed in bed,
bedclothes changed,
morning is more trouble
than all her seven decades.

She knows she's already left
a good part of this world.
She is scarcely able to speak,
yet reaches out her hand
when she hears the young nurse crying.

Easter

When the boy comes down from his room,
dressed in the dirty black
sweatshirt he's worn for weeks,
frayed sleeves pulled down over his wrists,

his father says he looks like an orphan,
says go upstairs and put on a tie.
His mother says, *No, stay,*
then asks that he offer the blessing.

At the table, his parents
bow their heads and close their eyes;
he watches them wait for the blessing
in deepening silence.

Then his voice, steady and sure,
speaks of the favor of grace,
only to falter when he sees on their faces
the words taking them to a place he cannot find.

The Button

Sitting
by the window,
eyes lowered,
the deaf woman
does not see
her baby
crying;

bathed in light,
she sews
a button,
mending
the shirt
cradled in her arms.

Rented Room, Second Floor

He lives next to a church,
an abandoned chapel,
empty inside
under a bell that never rings.

An abandoned chapel,
quiet at night, and still....
Under a bell that never rings,
locked doors and shuttered windows.

A quiet night, and still,
he sits on the balcony, listening:
locked doors and shadows,
a cross and crescent moon.

He sits on the balcony, listening.
Empty inside.
A cross and crescent moon.
He lives next to a church.

Sicily

Listen, I will tell you a mystery!
We will not all die,
but we will all be changed...

The woman was on her way
to the market in the square
to buy bread and fresh fish
for her husband and daughter

when she saw the mourners
dressed in black, weeping,
holding one another as they walked
down narrow stone streets

toward the cemetery. She drew back
as the pallbearers passed,
then joined the procession,
following, like the others in sorrow,

the polished wooden casket
carried through iron gates
past rows of headstones
to the open grave,

where the bereaved prayed
and offered flowers to the earth.
After the ceremony, the mourners
turned toward home,

leaving the woman
alone with the mystery
before she, too, turned
back to her daily tasks —

buying bread, buying fish,
feeding the living.

After the Storm

Favignana

At the height of the storm—
the midnight sky
ravished by lightning that blazed
and flashed
in rapid, blinding bursts—
candles burned inside the house
on a table strewn with poems.

In the quiet hour before dawn,
after the torrent had ebbed
and thunder had passed,
there came a ringing:
a jumble of sheep
advancing down the street,
tended by an old man and two boys,
the flock changing pastures,
bells about their necks so none would be lost.

Under a gray sky, the roof garden
lay in shambles. Below, in the harbor,
small fishing boats were setting out,
clearing the jetty, leaving the channel
for the open sea. The sky slowly cleared
as each boat struggled toward the horizon,
where, one after another, the vessels disappeared
into that blue where fishermen drop their nets.

The Ruined Church

This church is a dark ruin
built from ruins —

pillars scavenged from temples,
stones stolen from castles,

the benches, altar, and confessional
rescued from a modest chapel

long ago burned to the ground.
This house has suffered

earthquakes, flood, fire —
time's ravages. Still,

light shines
through the nave's high arches,

shimmering in cobwebs
that, luminous, shroud the broken windows.

Two Years after a Death

the Blue Ridge Mountains

Taking shelter in the cleft of a rock
on a cliff face lashed by rain,
I waited for lightning to pass
and thought of him, how suffering
is like rock, hard and bare.

When the clouds broke,
clear sky sparkled
beyond a gnarled oak
no bigger than a child.
Wind-blasted, storm-struck,
the oak jutted from the rock wall —
branches twisting toward sunlight,
thirsting roots driving deeper down, cracking
the stone it lives on.

A Light Rain

the Protestant Cemetery in Rome

Shelley's ashes
are buried in the *parte antica*
by the old wall under oaks on top of the hill,
next to his friend Trelawny.
A narrow path leads away from the rows
of tightly packed graves
and down steps to camellias
blossoming in a little meadow
where Keats lies,
Joseph Severn the only one beside him.
In his tiny room by the Spanish Steps,
Keats had rejoiced as he lay dying,
telling Severn he already could feel
the flowers growing over him —
wild daisies, white and blue violets.
How wonderful, he told his friend,
to be buried in a place so sweet.
But a cemetery's beauty
and a poet's words
could not console Severn,
and he fell sick with grief.
Now their damp stones glisten darkly
and violets fade beneath an overcast sky.
The path circles back
to the old part of the cemetery,
the many bodies.
Goethe's only son is buried here,

and William Wordsworth's grandson—
even three-year-old William Shelley
lies beside his father.

Son

Just after midnight, Andrew woke,
crying, struggling in the dark.
I lifted the tiny body from the crib,
whispered words of comfort.
But I could not console him.
He wanted to be held close
and rocked in his mother's arms.

The Artist

The painter painted his wife for years
in canvas after canvas: stepping from a bath,
her warm skin pink beneath a white towel,

sitting at a dressing table, her blue robe
loose and open as she dreamily combed her hair.
The artist worked tirelessly, as if her body held

the answer to a great mystery. She knew
her husband was fortunate to have married
one who trusted life completely, who embraced

each moment without thought, without words.
She was, she knew, a human being worthy
of the infinite awe and endless attention of another.

After all, the man could have married a shrew
and spent his life painting trees. Or dead birds,
slaughtered, and artfully arranged on the kitchen table.

On the Way to the Museum

It is possible, of course,
that you are not what you seem,
not as lovely as my mind needs to make you.
As you passed me on the corner near the Art Institute,
you turned your head away at the precise moment
I would have framed your face in my memory.
And now that you are gone forever,
I see only the broad and busy streets
filled with passing strangers I'll never meet.
I climb the wide stone stairs and enter the museum
to meditate on the immutable works of the long-lost dead.

The Rights of Man

I was outside in the cold,
Knocking on the window,
So I got up from my chair
And opened the door.

Painting William's Room

After emptying the white room,
we pry open a bucket of blue paint.
On the wall where the crib will go,
with one quick stroke I make
the dark outline of a woman
silhouetted against endless snow.
Laura's arm sweeps in long arcs—
a blue man emerges from her brush.
Blue woods rise from distant mists,
rivers flow to the sea, deep hues
of late autumn light fall over the world,
and the man and the woman
disappear into a single sky
which never shall be sundered and cannot die.

The Catcher's Mask

Before you were born, I hung it on a nail
on the blue wall above the waiting crib
like a good-luck charm to watch over you.
Your mother had me take it down.
She worried a mask would frighten you—
the empty face behind the metal cage.
But it's a mask from my youth,
the metal rusted, the straps cracked,
the leather padding soft as butter.
I've kept it, knowing one day
you will pull it on and it will shield you—
kneeling in the red dirt, waiting
for the pitches thrown at you.

Noon

The mind is a farmhouse far out on the otherwise
empty prairie, somewhere in Kansas or Nebraska.
Inside—a homemade bench and table, a grandfather's
four-poster bed, a modest study with books.
There are few possessions—a coffeepot,
a pair of work gloves, a sewing kit, a lantern.
The windows are plain, without curtains—
no one ever comes down this road.
A stairway leads to closed upper rooms
sparsely furnished and filled with light.
It is good sometimes to climb the stairs, to unlock
the doors and stand in one room after the other,
looking out the window to see things as they really are,
shadowless beneath a thousand miles of open sky.

The Sweater

This morning I bought a sweater made of fleece—
something soft to wear because life is hard.

At noon I sat on the kitchen floor with Andrew,
kissing him to make up for leaving the house
and making him cry.

After lunch, he took his nap.
I put on my new sweater, zipped it up,
and went outside and shoveled snow,
the flakes flying, white dust in the wind.

Then I came in and went down to my desk

and finally wrote the ending to a poem
I think I'll keep for myself, a poem
about a gold-lacquered, wooden statue—
a tenth-century Buddha, the hands broken off.

I hold out hands
that are empty and poor
like a beggar by the temple door.

Double Doors

Valentine's Day breakfast at Baker's Square:
Laura drinks coffee while I watch Andrew,
who refuses to sit but chooses instead
to stay in the restaurant's vestibule where
he opens and closes the big double doors
over and over again, as if he's practicing
a grand entrance—entering, crossing
the threshold, and letting the doors
close behind him. I'm thinking,

it wasn't so long ago I carried my tiny son
piggyback through the woods to a waterfall;
wasn't long ago I kissed Laura for the first time;
wasn't long ago I lived in the house with my dog
and sat with my notebook at the kitchen table
on Sunday morning after working all night—
sipping burnt coffee and scratching out lines,
lighting my hundredth cigarette, starting over
again, determined to write a love poem.

The Desk

All day writing poems, I was glad
to push away from my desk finally
like a ship setting sail, heading out
into the great and vast unknown,
which turned out to be dinner
with my son at Burger King,
my son who of late refuses to eat,
and whom I thought to tempt
with french fries and ketchup.
But how could I have known
that tonight I would drive the car
through town like a tour guide
pointing out the sights to Andrew,
who is suddenly obsessed
with the number six,
so that when I'd say *Clock tower,*
he'd say, *Six!,*
or when I'd say *Bookstore,*
he'd point and say, *Six!*
I knew we'd bathe before bed —
that's our ritual —
but was surprised when he didn't
need me to rock him to sleep:
he climbed straight into bed in the dark.
And I'd never have guessed, earlier today
when I was trying to write like a visionary,
that I'd go down to the laundry room
tonight, too tired for poetry,

open a bucket of red paint,
and paint the toddler desk and chair
bought last year at a rummage sale
so my son, too, would have a place to write.

The Fox

Driving home from work,
the dark coming early
to the city in the rain,
shops and newsstands
neglected and derelict
under the streetlamps,
the muted metronome
of the wiper blades
ticking away the time,
I saw a fox dashing
along the embankment,
racing the lights
of the commuter train
chugging through the mist.
The intelligent eyes,
the slender face,
the lithe body,
the reddish tail
darted under
a chain-link fence,
disappearing
into a small wilderness
of rubbish and weeds
growing wild in the grim
shadows of the underpass —
a small piece of divinity
vanishing from sight
beneath the tracks
that carry the Skokie Swift.

The Rock

Coming across some old poems today,
I smiled to think of the sad
young man I used to be,
always running off to Europe
like a poor monk on pilgrimage.
How many ancient churches did I kneel in,
listening to prayers in Latin?
How many days did I spend looking upward
into the vast empty spaces of great cathedrals,
the glory revealed
though I did not understand it?
I recall with fondness that young man I used to be,
the young man who once loved choirs
praising heaven in French and German,
who sat in the gardens of Villa Borghese
reading, "But I have lived
and have not lived in vain,"
believing I would live like Byron.
But now those wandering days
are over. I'm happy
to sit with Andrew on the cold ground
among leaves beneath bare trees,
thinking about that one round rock
in the middle of the stream that winds its way through our town —
that rock, with the silver water flowing over it.

The Ceiling Fan

Today I enjoyed
some privacy.
No visitors, no one
calling, nowhere to go.
A light snow
hesitated in the air —
drifting serenely.
Andrew and I put on our
blue coats, went out
for our morning walk.
Counted blackbirds.
The house was lonely
and still when we
returned. Later in the day,
as Andrew napped,
the afternoon lulled
into a deeper quiet.
I telephoned a florist
and sent flowers,
closing my eyes to
imagine the bouquet.
Then I lay down, too,
studying the ceiling fan,
wasting the afternoon,
doing nothing. Tomorrow
will be here soon enough.
My son will see
but not comprehend
the body lying still

The Blessing
377

among the peaceful
flowers. He'll see tears,
he'll see fresh dirt
black by the grave.
Today in our quiet house,
afternoon languidly passes,
the fan slowly spinning.
How little there is
to teach my son
about the art of living
equal to the wisdom
of loafing, spending the day
together, doing
nothing.

Golf Towels

Whenever my father visits,
he brings me golf towels
retrieved from the banks
of ditches lining fairways
or picked out of trash cans
in clubhouse parking lots.
What others pitch, he
takes home and launders—
rags to use around the house.

On my birthday he gave me
an entire box of towels—
one for each year of my life—
that he collected over the summer.
I unfolded each one slowly
before the assembled family
as my father told each towel's story
and explained each colorful logo.

For beauty
and intricacy of design,
we agreed the blue towel
emblazoned with the yellow crown
is the one we love, the blue towel
from the Old Course at St. Andrew's.
Almost too fine to use, Laura laid it
carefully on the kitchen table
like a priceless family heirloom.

Later that evening
while I bathed Andrew,
my mother, sister, and wife
sat together in the darkening garden,
a society apart,
their voices warm and intimate
below the open window.
I wrapped the small blue
towel with the yellow crown
around his glistening body
then handed Andrew to his grandfather,
who powdered and dressed him for bed.

Tree

When the sun goes down
I have my first drink
standing in the yard,
talking to my neighbor
about the alder tree
rising between our houses,
a lowly tree that prospered
from our steady inattention
and shot up quick as a weed
to tower over our rooftops,
where it now brandishes
a rich, luxuriant crown.
Should we cut it down?
Neither of us wants to—
we agree that we like
the flourishing branches,
shade like thick woods.
We don't say it,
studying our tree in silence,
but we know that if the roots
get into the foundations
we've got real trouble.
John goes back inside.
Nothing to be done in summer—
not to those heavy branches.
I balance my empty glass
on top of a fence post.
In the quiet early dark,
those peaceful minutes

before dinner, I bend down
to the flower beds I love
and pull a few weeds—
something I've meant to do
all day.

Rapture

a bedtime story, after Tolstoy

In the desert, a traveler
returning to his family
is surprised
by a wild beast.

To save himself
from the fierce animal,
he leaps into a deep well
empty of water.

But at the bottom
is a dragon, waiting
with open mouth
to devour him.

The unhappy man,
not daring to go out
lest he should be
the prey of the beast,

not daring to jump
to the bottom
lest he should be
devoured by the dragon,

clings to the branch
of a bush growing
in the cracks of the well.
Hanging upon the bough,

he feels his hands
weaken, yet still
he clings, afraid
of his certain fate.

Then he sees two mice,
one white, the other black,
moving about the bush,
gnawing the roots.

The traveler sees this
and knows that he must
inevitably perish, that he will
never see his sons again.

But while thus hanging
he looks about and sees
on the leaves of the bush
some drops of honey.

These leaves
he reaches with his tongue
and licks the honey off,
with rapture.

About the Author

Richard Jones was born in London, and raised in Virginia; he now lives in Evanston, Illinois, with his wife, Laura, and their sons, Andrew and William.

Index of Titles

The Blessing

Index of Titles

Index of First Lines

The Blessing

The Blessing

The Chinese character for poetry (*shih*) combines "word" and "temple."
It also serves as pressmark and raison d'être for Copper Canyon Press.

Founded in 1972, Copper Canyon Press remains dedicated to publishing
poetry exclusively, from Nobel laureates to new and emerging authors.
The Press thrives with the generous patronage of readers, writers, booksellers,
librarians, teachers, and students — everyone who shares the conviction
that poetry clarifies and deepens social and spiritual awareness.
We invite you to join this community of supporters.

For information and catalogs:

COPPER CANYON PRESS
Post Office Box 271
Port Townsend, Washington 98368
360/385-4925
poetry@coppercanyonpress.org
www.coppercanyonpress.org

This book is set in Sabon, designed by Jan Tschichold. In 1960, Tschichold was commissioned to create a typeface based on the types of Claude Garamond that would be interchangeable in both foundry type and mechanical composition. Tschichold understood the book production process very well—he was responsible for the design of Penguin Books from 1947–49. His technical and artistic skills combined to create a face that is handsome, highly readable, economical to set, and robust enough to stand up to the speed of web presses. Book design and composition by Valerie Brewster, Scribe Typography.

CPSIA information can be obtained at www.ICGtesting.com
Printed in the USA
LVOW06s0959180514

386019LV00006B/10/P

9 781556 591433